speculation /ˌspɛkjʊˈleɪʃən/

noun

• an act of speculating, or the result of this; a conclusion, opinion, view, or series of these, reached by abstract or hypothetical reasoning.

• contemplation of a profound, far-reaching, or subtle character; abstract or hypothetical reasoning on subjects of a deep, abstruse, or conjectural nature.

• a plan or scheme for some enterprise or undertaking.

• an act or instance of speculating; a commercial venture or undertaking of an enterprising nature, esp. one involving considerable financial risk on the chance of unusual profit.

IN THIS ISSUE

CASEY LANCE BROWN

PISCINARII

THE FISHPOND SPECULATORS OF ROME

Casey Lance Brown is a landscape futurist and visual artist. His research-based practice focuses on the unintended environmental consequences and spatial economics of resource extraction, migration, speculation, and automation. His accompanying photographic series have been awarded by Photoville's *The Fence* (2016) and Photolucida's *Critical Mass* (2020). He has held research positions at Harvard University Center for the Environment, Clemson University, and MIT's P-REX lab and is a fellow of the American Academy in Rome.

✛ REAL ESTATE, AQUACULTURE, ECONOMICS

The Roman Empire boasts several firsts in economic history – the first apartment blocks, the first shopping mall, and perhaps the first market economy. Once a market economy permits the relatively free fluctuation of prices, speculative investors arise to take advantage of potentially lucrative market movements. Naturally, in an agrarian-based economy like that of Rome, the target assets are likely to hew closely to the fruits of the land and sea. In fact, the modern term "fund" derives from the Latin word *fundus*, originally referring to a farming estate. Likewise, the roots of modern investment funds can be found in the agricultural and aquacultural estates of the Roman era. By tracing a mixture of textual and archaeological remnants, these estates begin to look like protean versions of contemporary speculation schemes like hedge funds, real estate flipping, and new market startups.

Elite Roman landowners profited from the land through a system of villas since at least 200 BCE. Traditionally, scholarship on Roman villas has largely been focused on their opulent accoutrements and architectural styles. However, in Roman times "villa" referred to both the land and buildings of an estate together with its productive output. Being a productive farmer held immense cultural and financial value for Romans.[1] This value was codified in the property requirement to become a senator, which stood at one million sesterces by the time of Augustus (roughly equivalent to being a multi-millionaire today). As the imperial conquests opened significant new lands and flooded the markets with slave labor, villa ownership mushroomed as an ideal mix of stable income, high profitability, and cultural clout for the patrician class.

Piscinarii

A new type of villa soon emerged that attracted an especially fervent investment class – the *villa maritima*. This villa typology merged the showy, architectural *villa urbana* with an artificial estuary built for aquacultural production. These new coastal enclaves united fresh fish and eel aquaculture with opulent retreats where fine dining halls and breezy loggia overlooked the water. In essence, they functioned like the first hedge fund mixed with prime real estate – an elite speculative investment expected to rise in value over time while continually producing income and status for the villa owner. Interest in the *villa maritima* was so great that Roman writers mockingly named the owners *piscinarii*, or fishpond lovers.[2]

The multiple mentions by the primary Roman agricultural chroniclers, including Varro, Pliny the Elder, and Columella, denote the immense value placed on aquacultural estates. Stand out accounts include stories of Sergius Orata, who likely obtained his name from the fish that he grew, the gilt-head bream (also spelled *aurata* meaning "golden"). Mr. "Golden Fish-head" expanded his wealth by inventing methods for heating thermal spa baths installed in villas and for building artificial oyster beds in estuarine lakes to supply fresh shellfish to the very same villas.[3] Pliny the Elder notes that the famed General Lucullus had a tunnel dug through mountains to ensure his Neapolis fishponds received constant water circulation.[4] Some conclude that Lucullus's fortunes came to financial ruin due to his extensive pond works and villa expenditures.[5] Cornelia, the daughter of General Sulla, bought a prime villa on Capo Miseno for 300,000 sesterces and later sold it to Lucullus for 10 million.[6] Historical recorded transactions such as these mark villa owning as an elite activity. With new technology, coastal villa aquaculture elevated mere gentlemanly farming to an unparalleled investor class. And Varro, the preeminent Roman agricultural scholar, remarked that there may be more money to be made in aquaculture than in agriculture.[7]

Without movement and trade, the coastal villa outputs would remain local and perhaps not reach the storied letters of Rome's literati. Loans and standard contracts for shipping maritime commodities suggest that long-distance trade occurred with regularity. In addition, the investment loans for maritime trade could be very large in scale. One documented papyrus noted a value of 6,926,852 sesterces – seven times the property

TUSCANY

UMBRIA

ROME

LATIUM

S. Marinella

Ostia

Tyrrhenian Sea

Antium

Circeo

Sperlonga

Pontine Islands

threshold to become a Roman senator.[8] Also, there were pooled equity capital ventures called "societas" that acted as a kind of protean private equity fund. These are known to have been active in maritime commerce, but it is not known whether this activity was directly linked to villa aquacultural production.[9]

Critically, we know from Varro that the vast ancient sums handed over for the coastal villas partially derived from their *piscium multitudinem* [abundant fish], exemplified by a prominent eel farmer who sold his estate for four million sesterces.[10] Columella dedicated an entire book to explaining how to economically design and manage a proper aquacultural operation. His advice for aspiring coastal villa owners included hydrological and ichthyological details about water temperature, species compatibility, and artificial habitat enhancements – all in the interest of delivering financial gain through profit and marketability. For example, he recommended species-specific food and freshwater influx to induce weight gain for the farmed fish to ensure the higher price normally reserved for wild-caught seafood.[11] Columella's advice suggests aquacultural works had advanced to a high level of sophistication and economic importance by the first century CE.

Piscinae

Because Roman aquacultural pioneers developed highly robust underwater structures to house their prized fish, eels, and lampreys, the physical remnants of their enterprise are still visible today. Rock-cut terraces and structured basins made with a type of hydraulic concrete feature right along the Tyrrhenian coast of Italy and nearby islands. The sheer number attests to the magnitude of the ancient market for building, owning, and operating aquacultural operations. The actual piscinae [pools] are so well preserved that archaeologists have attempted to calculate the potential production of the aquacultural operations. Taking into consideration the water inputs, temperature, and potential capacities, one study estimated the largest known fishpond at Torre Astura could produce in excess of 50,000 kg of fish.[12] This output vastly exceeds the likely domestic consumption of the villa's inhabitants and implies export to the open Roman market or provisioning for imperial banquets. We also know that some Roman vessels had *vivaria* [live fish tanks] and, possibly, oxygenation pumps, which would enable vendors to keep the fish alive until they reached distant ports or market locations.[13]

Advanced features of various fishponds around the Mediterranean included highly ordered enclosures, careful orientation to the tidal flows, and aqueducts to improve freshwater influx [known to increase fish production through higher levels of dissolved oxygen]. The various rectangular enclosures, exedras, and symmetrical layouts could almost be mistaken for the plan of a Roman basilica. Much like the mysteries of the Pantheon's function and oculus, we do not know precisely how the various basins, channels, and divisions

were utilized. Perhaps the divisional structures managed the various ages and species of fish and eels, including their graduated salinity needs.

The Villa of Tiberius at Sperlonga indicates that habitat preferences were considered in the design of piscinae. Ceramic vessels remain visible in the constructed piscina walls, acting as an artificial version of the reef habitat where moray eels are traditionally found. Columella clearly specified matching conditions in the piscinae for rock-dwelling fishes so that they might "feel their captivity as little as possible."[14] Incredibly, fish still populate many of these pools. North of Rome, the remains of a *villa maritima* known as Punta della Vipera continue to attract fisherman who stalk various prey among the Roman aquacultural works to this day.

Prima Facie

The 2,000-year durability of Roman piscinae provides an instructive anchoring point for speculative episodes that propagated in more recent history. New logistical technologies that open access to a marketable commodity have long driven speculative bubbles in advanced economies. In the colonial era, transoceanic ship access underpinned the Mississippi Company and South Sea Company land-rush bubbles. In the 19th century, railways kickstarted several speculative commodity bubbles in Europe and the US, and in the 20th century highways were catalysts for speculative housing developments in suburban regions.

Rome's extravagant estate investment bears remarkable similarity to these periodic bubbles. It operated in a nascent market economy that was perhaps the first to develop the spatial sophistication to grow a speculative bubble. Roman markets were filled with tradeable goods from the edges of its empire, such as salted tuna from Spain and metals from Britain. Astute fishpond designers from the Roman era established methods for concentrated production of the estuarine species, nearshore species, and eel species using natural stock and precise control of the intertidal zone. Likely, these new products could then be transported by boat to coastal cities and up the Tiber River to Rome itself. Hundreds of senators, generals, and other patricians would likely desire owning such a productive asset. With the newfound wealth and slave labor extracted from empire expansion, the perfect conditions were set for every aspiring villa developer to exploit the resource. The scale of the aquacultural pools, the technological spread, the frequency that villas changed hands, and the growing urban markets for the freshest seafood all make a prima facie case for the investment value of these sites.

Today, vast wealth accumulation and sudden consumer access have inflated market bubbles in new areas like cryptocurrencies, meme stocks, and dubious internet startups. Unlike these digitally fabricated targets, Roman villa investors were collaborating with tangible, natural systems to concentrate an in-demand, luxury

food commodity. Fresh fish was highly valued in the markets and banquets of Rome, especially during the more inclement seasons of the Mediterranean when fishing was difficult. By the second century CE, Rome's urban population success had outgrown the natural food supply of its immediate hinterland and it thus depended on food imported from elsewhere. The Roman senatorial class, legally restricted from participating in direct commercial activities like banking and international trade, would have seen this market need as the perfect match for their valuable villas. They were required to justify their wealth through some type of societally useful production[15] and marine aquaculture offered a new technology that fed their own status banquets and augmented their villa-based wealth.

In a market where a single, fresh surmullet (a fish species that dramatically changes color as it dies) could sell for 1,200 sesterces, patricians found a lucrative overlap between a prestige property, a new technology, and a marketable commodity. By partnering with natural tides and ecological niches, they designed an asset that offered both speculative and durational value. The only comparable investment targets that meet these criteria today might be agriculture, biotechnology, and extraterrestrial mining ventures. After the financial crisis in 2008, bundled farmland assets attracted pension fund managers, like TIAA and Sweden's National Pension Fund, and private investors like Bill and Melinda Gates and the Harvard Management Company. This strategy capitalized on the notion that quality farmland assets tend to be countercyclical: holding or rising when the regular stock market drops. Concurrently, the billionaire investment mania is clearly fixated on the logistical and status-elevating potentials of space (as evidenced by SpaceX, Blue Origin, and Virgin Galactic). Farmland assets and space ventures both have the potential for long-term rises in value regardless of the vacillations in quotidian markets.

Viewed from the 2,000-year-old Roman perspective, these investments make perfectly rational, speculative sense. Urban populations are expanding globally with a parallel demand for global food commodities. Farmland for food production, rare earth minerals for technological production, and clean air, land, and water remain finite resources on Earth. With the excess capital accumulating to a new class of tech elite, an investment case could be made for sea-based, orbital, or lunar real estate as the next frontier in exclusive development. The Romans might call these investors the *lunarii* – an appropriate label given its shared Latin root with the noun "lunatic."

1 Annalisa Marzano, *Roman Villas in Central Italy: A Social and Economic History* (Brill, 2007), 85.

2 Cicero, *Letters to Atticus*, trans. D. R. Shackleton Bailey, Loeb Classical Library 7 (Harvard University Press, 1999), I.20, I.19, II.9.

3 William Smith (ed.), *Dictionary of Greek and Roman Antiquities*, vol. 3 (C. Little, and J. Brown, 1870), 40.

4 Pliny the Elder, *The Natural History*, trans. John Bostock & H.T. Riley (Taylor and Francis, 1855), Book IX, 80.

5 José Fernandez Polanco, "Aquaculture Production and Marketing in the Roman Empire," *FAO Aquaculture Newsletter* 59 (2018): 55–56.

6 Marzano, *Roman Villas in Central Italy*, 77.

7 Ursula Rothe, "The Roman Villa: Definitions and Variations," in Annalisa Marzano & Guy P.R. Métraux (eds), *The Roman Villa in the Mediterranean Basin: Late Republic to Late Antiquity* (Cambridge University Press, 2018), 46.

8 Peter Temin, *The Roman Market Economy* (Princeton University Press; Reprint ed., 2017), 172.

9 Dominic Rathbone, "The Financing of Maritime Commerce in the Roman Empire, I-II AD" in Elio Lo Cascio (ed.), *Credito e Moneta nel Mondo Romano* (Edipuglia, 2003), 197–229.

10 Marcus Terentius Varro, "De Re Rustica, 3.17.3," quoted in Marzano, *Roman Villas in Central Italy*, 14.

11 Polanco, "Aquaculture Production and Marketing in the Roman Empire," 56.

12 Annalisa Marzano & Giulio Brizzi, "Costly Display or Economic Investment? A Quantitative Approach to the Study of Roman Marine Aquaculture," *Journal of Roman Archaeology* 22 (2009): 225.

13 Marzano & Brizzi, "Costly Display or Economic Investment?" 227.

14 Columella, *On Agriculture*, vol. I, Books 1–4, trans. Harrison Boyd Ash, Loeb Classical Library 361 (Harvard University Press, 1941), 8.17.6.

15 Heather Pringle, "How Ancient Rome's 1% Hijacked the Beach," *Hakai Magazine: Coastal Science and Societies* (April 5, 2016), https://www.hakaimagazine.com/features/how-ancient-romes-1-hijacked-beach/.

Acknowledgments
Original research and travel generously supported by the American Academy in Rome and the Prince Charitable Trusts Rome Prize.

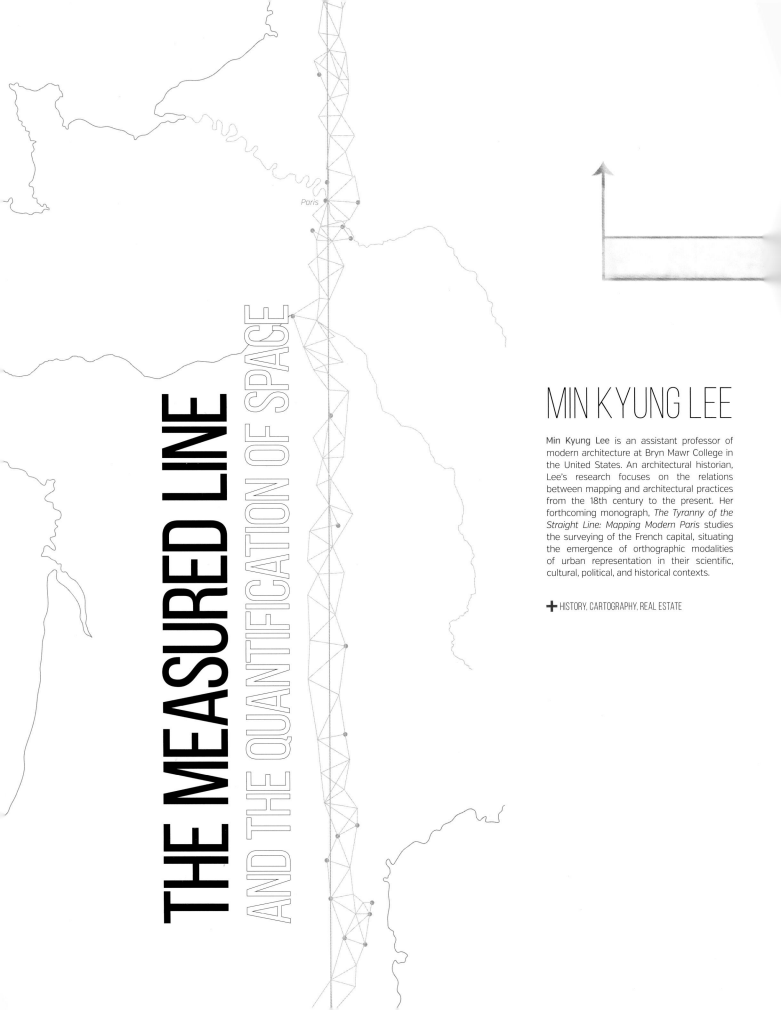

THE MEASURED LINE
AND THE QUANTIFICATION OF SPACE

Paris

MIN KYUNG LEE

Min Kyung Lee is an assistant professor of modern architecture at Bryn Mawr College in the United States. An architectural historian, Lee's research focuses on the relations between mapping and architectural practices from the 18th century to the present. Her forthcoming monograph, *The Tyranny of the Straight Line: Mapping Modern Paris* studies the surveying of the French capital, situating the emergence of orthographic modalities of urban representation in their scientific, cultural, political, and historical contexts.

+ HISTORY, CARTOGRAPHY, REAL ESTATE

Look at any real estate advertisement today and a price per square meter is clearly marked. It is determined by the total price of a property divided by its occupiable area. The link between price and a unit of surface area is foundational in assessing value within a global property market. Necessarily reductive, this description homogenizes differing qualities of a given space to its quantitative measure. Precisely because these differences are flattened, the price per square meter allows for property to be abstracted; compared to and exchanged for another regardless of differences in location, material, or character. This transferability depends on the consistency of one unit of measure; while the price will necessarily fluctuate in a market-driven economy, surface area measures stay constant in this economic formula. The invariability of the meter (or square footage, depending on the country) across all spaces is fundamental to the financial speculation associated with property.

This essay describes the meter's determination and adoption while considering the political and social values associated with this now-universal measure. Central to the meter's formulation was an attempt to quantify space that began in earnest during the Enlightenment. Yet, while this measure was born out of historically specific conditions to measure the world, it became understood as objective and impartial because of how it was visually depicted. That is, the specific modes of the meter's graphic representation became a crucial element in projecting its universality. The plan, which is now ubiquitous as an instrument of spatial representation, makes possible forms of financial speculation on physical property as it flattens differences in character and quality down to a reductive measure of quantity. Thus, the claim in this text is twofold. First, the quantification of space and the adoption of a universal measure was not neutral. And second, the political values that were embedded in these measures were obscured by the particular representational language–the orthographic plan–that developed in parallel with these political and economic concerns.

1 Witold Kula, *Measure and Men*, trans. R. Szreter (Princeton University Press, 1986), 29.

2 John Bender & Michael Marrinan, *The Culture of Diagram* (Stanford University Press, 2010).

3 Min Kyung Lee, "An Objective Point of View: the orthogonal grid in 18th-century plans of Paris," *The Journal of Architecture* 17, no. 1 (February 2012): 11–32.

4 In 1812, Napoleon returned France to the old standards and then, in the 1840s, Louis Philippe reinstated the metric system.

5 Delambre was to survey the northern section from Dunkirk to Rodez Cathedral, and Méchain the southern section from Rodez Cathedral to Montjüic Fortress near Barcelona.

6 Dated as 22 June 1799. Today, the true or invariable meter is defined as a length equal to 1,650,763.73 wavelengths of the orange light emitted by the Krypton atom of mass 86 *in vacuo*. Delambre and Méchain's triangulation survey suffered many interruptions due to revolutionary events, and even when the survey had been officially cancelled in 1795 and after Méchain's death, Delambre continued through 1799. There were also mistakes that were made by Méchain in his survey around Barcelona, which led to delays. For a full account, see Ken Alder, *The Measure of All Things: The Seven-year Odyssey and Hidden Error that Transformed the World* (Free Press, 2002).

7 Ken Alder, "Making Things the Same: Representation, Tolerance and the End of the Ancien Regime in France," *Social Studies of Science* 28, no. 4 (1998): 499–545.

8 For a definition of precision and accuracy, see "Introduction," in Wise M. Norton (ed.), *The Values of Precision* (Princeton University Press, 1995), 3–14.

9 Kula suggests that every moment of metrological standardization has been associated with absolutism. See Kula, *Measure and Men*, 115.

On 1 August 1793, the meter–defined as one-ten-millionth of the distance from a pole to the equator–was mandated as the standard measure in France, the first country to adopt the metric system. This was a profound shift that would affect all aspects of society, uprooting fundamentally accepted norms of social relations and political life. Until this time in Europe, the measurement of land was based on, as Witold Kula describes, human relations to the land and the land's fertility. Thus, cultivated land was measured by the input of labor, the type of cultivation, and the quantity of seed required to make it productive.[1] During the Ancien Régime, different trades employed different systems of measurement or quantification, creating a dense and intricate web of anthropometric values with variations based on personal negotiations, artisanal practices, local regions, and even specific rulers. Units of measure were qualitatively determined, and in this way, almost all pre-modern measures were defined locally. Subsequent attempts to quantify space meant translating qualities that had formerly been described in units specific to particular bodies, temporalities, and sites into new universally accepted numeric quantities. These numbers were represented abstractly through graphic systems, such as triangulation and coordinate tables that were not concerned with specific materiality but rather with reproducibility. The measured drawing was an ambitious attempt to rationalize space into a geometric grid, which in large part succeeded.

Efforts to quantify space had a direct and profound effect on how cities were represented. Maps–which had previously rendered urban space pictorially or perspectivally, highlighting the profile and character of a place–began to be drawn orthographically by the end of the 18th century, with blocks and roads represented principally in plan. This shift resulted in a map's accuracy no longer being evaluated by the pictorial verisimilitude between image and terrain but by its geometric correspondence. With the shift from the perspectival to the orthographic, the map sacrificed pictorial legibility and became aligned with a growing and broader diagrammatic culture, most extensively manifest in Diderot and Delambert's *Encyclopédie*.[2] The scientific iconography of diagrams emptied the page of human figures and reduced all relations to measured, reproducible lines. The measured plan, for example, offered an image that could be consumed in a single glance. This ease of consumption contributed to the plan's status as objective because it assumed no mediation – its information was immediately apparent.[3] It was not a representation that offered depth and unfolded across pictorial space, revealing different elements over time. Rather, the orthographic plan, diagrammatic in its composition, equalized all lines onto the surface of the page, assuming an atemporal and decontextualized space. Moreover, with a grid aligned to the meter, it produced a measured map that could claim universal applicability.

The determination of this new quantitative measure, land surveying, and mapmaking were inseparable. In 1791, Charles-Maurice de Talleyrand and Marie-Jean-Antoine-Nicolas Condorcet offered legislation for a national standard for measures, which was eventually adopted by the revolutionary government based on economic grounds.[4] The French National Constituent Assembly charged the task of the meter's ground survey to the astronomers Jean-Baptiste-Joseph Delambre and Pierre-Francois-Andre Méchain, who set out from the Paris Observatory that same year.[5] Using the surveying methods of triangulation, the aim was to define the base line of the meridian through Paris to which all other maps would refer, and to create a standardized and relational system of distances and measures contingent upon neither human relations nor the human body. Instead, this was a measure defined by a planetary reference, the earth's meridian, and would alter the value of space from the qualitative to the quantitative.[6]

The change in units of measurements from various local systems to a single metric system had two goals: first, to facilitate the free exchange of goods by introducing a uniform means of comparing and defining them; and secondly, to enable the government to generate and collect accurate information about its resources. The adoption and use of a universal unit of measure held the ideological promise of equality. It presented a new logic motivated by, as Condorcet and Talleyrand claimed, the facilitation of circulation and exchange.[7] The metric measure assumed a flattened and gridded (Euclidean) space, through which material exchange—goods or land— could easily be conducted. Moreover, by translating the object and site to its metric measures, it separated them from their environmental, social, historical, and cultural contexts. Maps that now used the meter scale related to each other through a network based on the shared reference of the meridian rather than the subjectivity of a local context. By constructing a standard cartographic description around the surveyed meridian and a meter—both defined in relation to one another—graphic representation was equated to spatial reality.[8]

In addition to arguments for a standard measure grounded in economic exigencies and the ideal of equality, they were also intimately tied to France's imperial aims.[9] Napoleon Bonaparte's campaign in Egypt (1789–1801) became central to testing these new methods and measures of surveying and mapping. More than 150 scholars accompanied the soldiers on this mission, and while Bonaparte's military ambitions

ultimately failed, the expedition did produce the 22-volume *Description de l'Egypte* – a monumental study of Egypt's geography, history, and culture published between 1809 and 1822. A section devoted to Egypt's topography was intended to be the study's chief contribution, representing the major work that was undertaken by the expedition's scientific mission. The goal had been to measure the arc of the meridian in latitudes south of France, as well as to cover Egypt in a chain of primary and secondary triangles that would link first to Corsica and then ultimately back to France.[10] In the end, due to the resistant local conditions—both climatic and political—as well as the sinking of the ship "Patriote" with its surveying equipment, a comprehensive survey was impossible to realize.[11] Only specific local areas were triangulated and then compiled from diverse manuscript maps using astronomical control points. Surveying was limited to the Nile and the extent of its seasonal floods, the location of wells and canals and other waterways, and coastlines of particular defensive concern.

In the last year of the expedition, General Menou shifted surveying priority to cadastral mapping in order to undermine and usurp the Coptic monopoly of taxation and appropriate much-needed funds by replacing the *iltizam* system, based on feudal hierarchies, with a direct tax on land.[12] In order to gain control of the land revenues, the French were interested in eliminating the intermediaries who collected taxes from the peasantry on behalf of the Ottomans.[13] On March 1, 1801, the Cadastral Commission of Egypt was convened, and the ways in which the cadaster should be conducted were discussed.[14] However, with military defeat imminent, the French surveyors were not able to realize their objectives, as they could only reach places that the accompanying soldiers could defend. The variability of the surveying conditions and the inability to access certain areas is

10 There are no surviving archival records that document at what stage and by whom the triangulated survey was decided. Godlewska speculates that it was Napoleon himself and that the decision was made in France. Based on Huguenin's study of mapping Corsica, a report was apparently sent by Lalande and Gaspard Monge that advised the *Carte Topographique de Corse* be engraved at 1:86,400 in order to link to the Cassini map of France, which was of the same scale. Godlewska speculates that it was Gaspard Monge who also suggested that the Egyptian survey use the same scale in order that all the surveys and maps of the entire Mediterranean region could relate. See Anna Godlewska, "Map, Text, Image: The Mentality of Enlightened Conquerors: A New Look at the *Description de l'Egypte*," *Transactions of the Institute of British Geographers* 20 [1995]: 5.

11 Charles Coulston Gillispie, "Scientific Aspects of the French Egyptian Expedition, 1798–1801," *Proceedings of the American Philosophical Society* 133, no. 4 [1989]: 467.

12 While there were different forms that the *iltizam* system took, in general, it was a method of state tax collection that was outsourced to a *mültazim*, often a noble, who was allowed to keep part of the tax revenue for himself. This greatly benefited the aristocracy who controlled not only the labor of peasants but also the amount owed to the state. For a broader discussion, see Carl F. Petry [ed.], *The Cambridge History of Egypt* [Cambridge University Press, 2008], 130. See also Stanford Shaw, "Landholding and Land-tax Revenues in Ottoman Egypt," *Political and Social Change in Modern Egypt* [Oxford University Press, 1968], 91–103.

13 Godlewska, "Map, Text, Image," 8–9.

14 Minutes of the Meeting of the Cadastral Commission [March 3, 1801], Paris, BNF, Mss Fr. 11275, Doc 93: 90–101.

15 Edme Francois Jomard, *Mémoire sur le Système Métrique des Anciens Égyptiens: Contenant des recherches sur leurs connaissances géométriques et sur les mesures des autres peuples de l'antiquité* [Paris, 1817], 699.

completely absent from what was ultimately presented as the cartographic image of Egypt's terrain.

Emphasized in the *Description de l'Egypte* was the colonial territory's connection to the metropole of Paris. Distances between sites in Egypt and the Paris meridian were marked on the corner of every map sheet, as well as on a chart, making a clear cartographic case for Egypt as part of French territorial claims. The Paris Observatory, a symbol of scientific progress, served as the anchor for the meridian, but its equivalent in Egypt was the pyramid of Giza, an asynchronous choice associating the country with the past. Significantly, the authority of these maps was located in their claim to geometric measurement and methods of quantification. In his *Mémoire sur le Système Métrique*, Edmé-Francois Jomard, director of the *Description de l'Egypte*, wrote, "Geometry, more than any other branch of knowledge, offers the means of achieving truth. In effect, the theorems of geometry do not allow vague interpretations to hold."[15] Geometry—and accordingly, its graphic expression—was understood as an unmediated path. It reduced the world to lines, incorruptible by human errors and fallacies, and offered clarity where there was none.

In making possible exchange between distant places and strangers, the meter represented a new spatial order that ignored context.[16] It did not matter if the terrain was city or countryside, inhabited or uninhabited, desert or forest, Egypt or France. The meter's definition and adoption thus justified France's colonial interests in the name of equality, efficiency, and exchange, disregarding difference. When used to determine a given area, the measured line permitted its representation to correspond proportionally to a metric grid that now marked the surface of the earth.[17] Ultimately, the meter was not an end in itself, but an instrument to extend France's control into new territories using a claim of universality. The possibilities of this universal measure signaled a new social order that sought to transform the feudal society into an imperial one, rationalizing the conquest of the

Egyptian territory and the subjugation of its people through a measured line. This same standard had consequences within France during the 19th century, when an urban middle class emerged through the real estate speculations of major urban renewal projects using the economic logic sustained by the meter. If earlier arguments for the metric system during the Enlightenment proposed an optimistic future of equality, mobility, and commerce, by the 19th century those expectations had settled into lines that demarcated spaces specifically for the bourgeoisie.[18] The universal measure had become a tool to secure political power.

In his definition of surveying in the supplement to the *Encyclopedie*, Condorcet argued that geometry and its use by surveyors could overcome social and political conflict.[19] Yet, ultimately, it was the reverse: geometry and its claims to universality inscribed and justified new forms of power. The political negotiations and military conquests that were central to the formulations of these numbers and lines, as well as the construction of their correspondence to a terrain, persist in current practices of financial speculations and their representations. Space is reduced to nothing more than surface area, and the particular qualities of its context and history–unable to be quantified and represented graphically–are discarded.[20] The contemporary devotion to data–measured lines and numbers–continues to feed into a self-reinforcing system in which "value" is determined universally and constitutes an economic market that conditions the future of a place and a people without representational recourse.

16 See Antoine Picon, *Architectes et Ingénieurs au Siècle des Lumières* (Parenthèses, 1988), 97.

17 Charles Coulston Gillispie, *Science and Polity in France: The Revolutionary and Napoleonic Years* (Princeton University Press, 2014), 223–85.

18 David Harvey, Paris: *Capital of Modernity* (Routledge, 2005).

19 Nicolas de Condorcet, "L'Arpentage" in *Supplément à l'Encyclopédie ou Dictionnaire Raisonné des Sciences, des Arts et des Métiers*, Vol. 1 (Chez M.M. Rey, 1776–1777), 567.

20 Paul Alliès, *L'invention du Territoire* (Presses Universitaires de Grenoble, 1980).

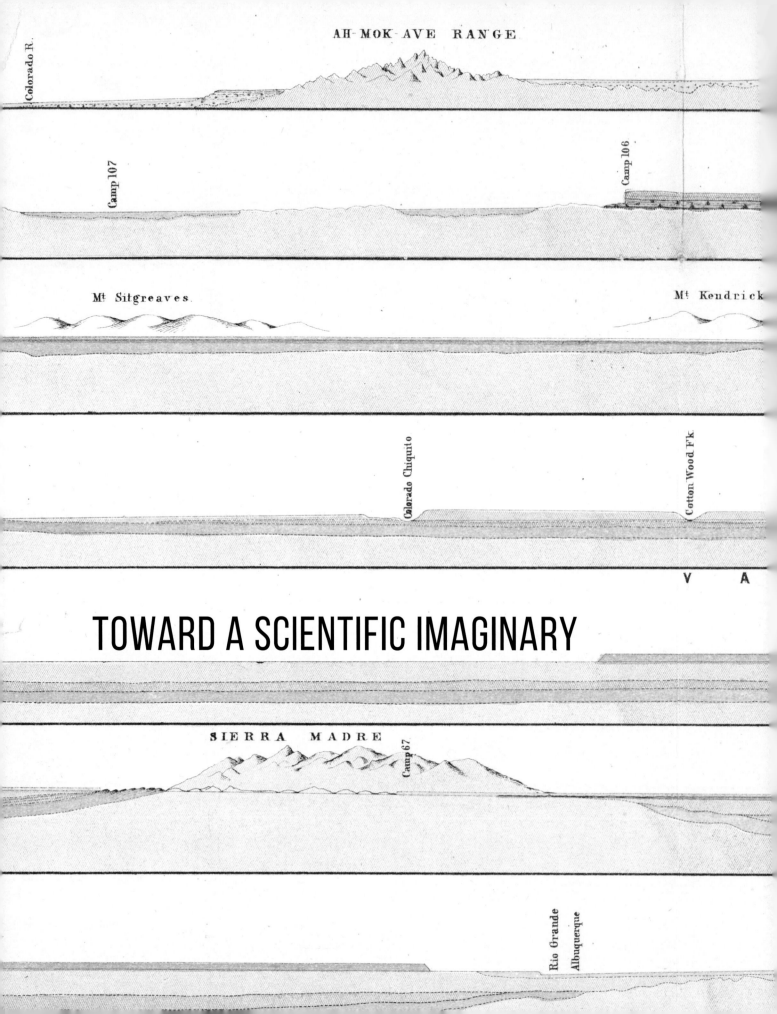

TOWARD A SCIENTIFIC IMAGINARY

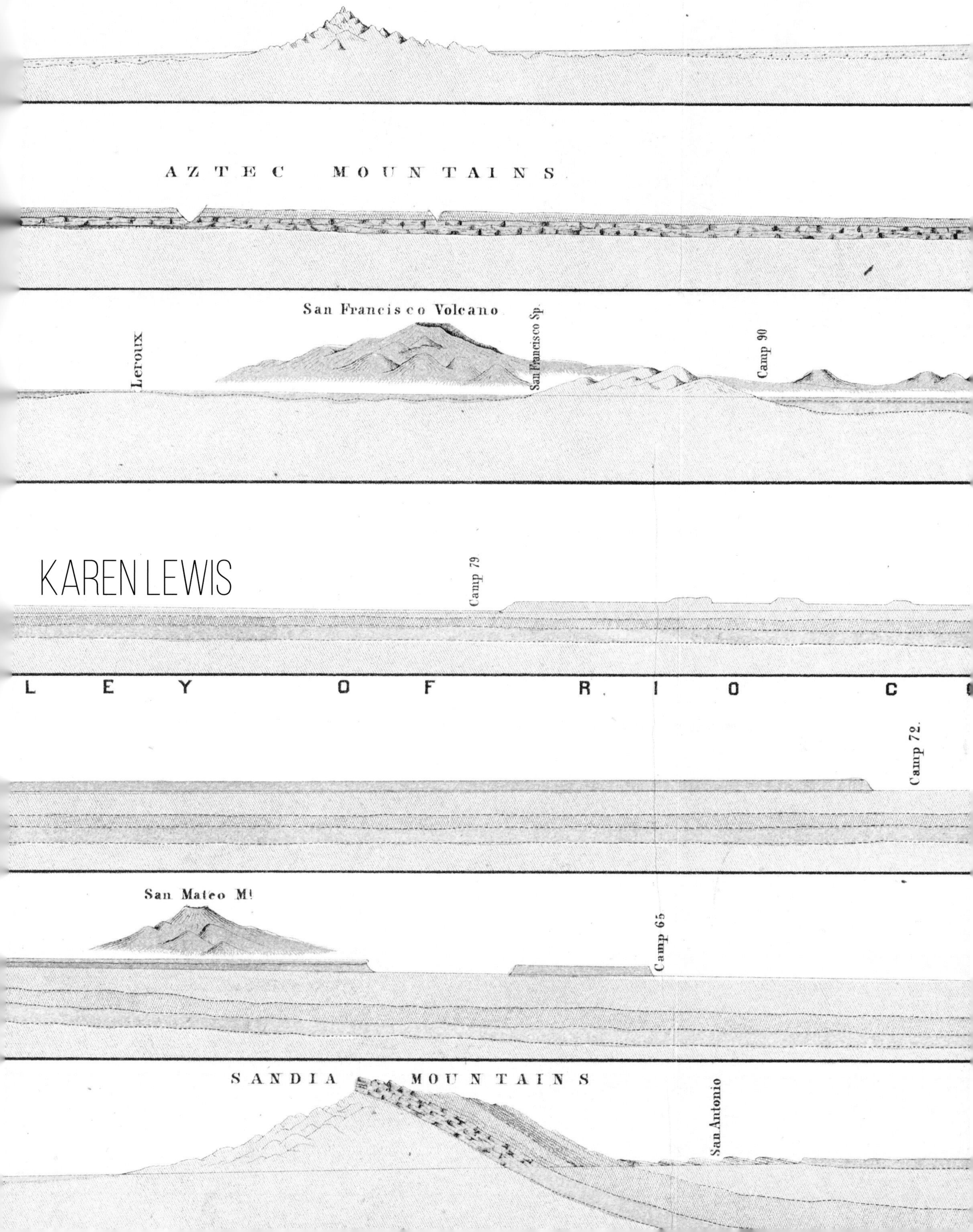

AZTEC MOUNTAINS.

San Francisco Volcano.

Leroux

San Francisco Sp.

Camp 90

KAREN LEWIS

Camp 79

L E Y   O F   R I O   C

Camp 72.

San Mateo Mt

Camp 65

SANDIA MOUNTAINS

San Antonio

Karen Lewis is an associate professor of architecture at the Ohio State University. A visualization specialist, Lewis's research explores the intersection of graphic and infrastructural systems with her recent work centering on the intricate maps, drawings, and diagrams of the Trans-Mississippi West. She is a graduate of Harvard University Graduate School of Design and Wellesley College and is author of *Graphic Design for Architects* (2015).

✚ CIVIL ENGINEERING, CARTOGRAPHY, GRAPHIC DESIGN

Science and engineering-based representations are often presumed to be purely objective expressing, in as accurate means as possible, the characteristics of particular observed phenomenon. Yet these representations are, in reality, often highly subjective – reliant on active forms of both speculation and interpretation. This is true in terms of the motivations behind their undertaking, but also in the methods of recording used. The story of the Corps of Topographical Engineers' ("the Topographic Corps") preparatory work on potential routes of the transcontinental railroad is notable in this regard.

An initiative motivated by political, economic, and scientific aspirations, the visual records of this undertaking are remarkable for both what they record and how they recorded it, but also for what other possibilities these visual records enabled. The story of the Topographic Corps that follows can be understood as a story of speculation in three parts: speculation by the Corps in the making of maps, diagrams, and other visual recordings; speculation by the patrons of these endeavors in assessing and interpreting the findings of the Corps; and, eventually, financial speculation by the broader public on land and real estate as the transcontinental railroad was constructed. This essay will focus on the first of these speculations in seeding the ground for the other two. That is, what follows is a consideration of the visual landscape vocabulary of the Topographic Corps in the production of a scientific imaginary.

For 25 years, between 1838 and 1863, the Topographic Corps operated as a small branch of the US Army. Comprising no more than 36 officers at any given time, the Topographic Corps was an elite group of Westpoint-trained soldier-engineers tasked with two principal activities. First, they supervised the surveying, engineering, and construction of new infrastructure projects. Acting as a type of mid-19th-century public works agency and precursor to the Army Corps of Engineers,[1] the Topographic Corps laid out national boundaries, located and constructed roads, dredged and removed snags from the Mississippi River, and built monuments, canals, and aqueducts. Topographic engineers were specifically trained in surveying and cartography. Their unique education differentiated them from field officers and the already novel Westpoint-trained military engineer, who had graduated from the first civil engineering curriculum in the United States. The Topographic Corps' unique representation skills led to a second—and primary—activity: to map, assemble, and visualize scientific information about the Trans-Mississippi West.

The expertise of the Topographic Corps was especially urgent during the mid-19th century in the United States. In less than three years, between 1846 and 1849, the whole country had been enlarged and reformed, marking a time of "enormous spatial change in the extent, shape, and geography of the United States of America."[2] The acquisition of new land occurred with the emergence of the railroad as a space-conquering technology. For several years, Congress was stymied by deeply contentious debates about where to build the transcontinental railroad. Questions remained about which states the new infrastructure would pass through, which ports and cities it would first connect, and which economies, land owners, and investors would most profit. The debates over these issues produced intense political gridlock, stalling the project for years. To move the discussion forward, Congress appropriated funding for four separate surveys of potential railroad routes through the West. These were to be conducted under the Secretary of War, Jefferson Davis, with the Topographic Corps executing the surveying work.

As was popular at the time, government looked to science to determine a policy for the West.[3] The Topographic Corps would study the interior, gathering information about conditions along each alternative route. They were to survey the landscape conditions from the Mississippi River to the Pacific to "ascertain the most practical, economical, national, and equitable" route possible. Rather than propose specific mile-by-mile grading plans for the railroad, the Topographic Corps was charged with amassing an abundance of generalized data through this reconnaissance. The Corps would draw profiles of each route, measuring the topography, elevation, and potential costs of building along each latitude. They would collect data on weather, precipitation, heat, wind, and other meteorological information. Detailed perspective drawings of landscape vistas were to accompany the collection, as were classifications of reptiles, fish, mammals, and birds. The reports would assess the available lumber, geology, aquifers, and other resources needed to construct the railroad. The hope was that by surveying the territory with an eye toward practicality and

feasibility, a natural and obvious solution would be found. Impartial science would break political passions and provide a comprehensive understanding of—and collection of speculative futures concerning—the unknown West.

In 1855, the Topographic Corps organized into seven parties – four parties explored potential railroad routes at different latitudes across the continent while the remaining three parties sought connections between the four routes. Sponsored by competing politicians from different states, each parallel became an argument for which cities to connect, which geographically related economic system to back, and which communities would ultimately most benefit from the railroad. The officers of the Corps were augmented with scientific experts from both the US and Europe. In total, 106 topographers, geologists, botanists, surgeons, meteorologists, and naturalists assembled[4] to study the proposed routes, compiling the massive scientific volumes of the *Pacific Railroad Reports*.

The 10 months of surveying represented the combined efforts of the Topographic Corps and a sizable contingent of the country's foremost scientists, including the research expertise from the newly formed Smithsonian Institution, which supplied instruments and established measuring techniques and research methods for the expeditions. The partnership between the Smithsonian and the government was strategic: an incredible influx of data about the West would flood into the Smithsonian,[5] helping to develop an institution on par with the more-established European scientific institutes. This partnership between science and military expertise, topographic measuring, and representations of nature, complicated the mission of the project because it split the role of the topographical engineer into two parts. As military men and scientifically educated engineers, Corps members were trained to assemble and organize the sights encountered into logical, systemic projections. But at the same time, their work wasn't just to explore, but to report back to Washington in a critical and projective way; describing what they encountered and making a case for a particular route over others. One can see this tension played out across the drawings – which in the case of the geological drawings, use similar representation techniques to the more common engineering profiles. Notably, the drawings in question are far less precise and far more interpretive, even fanciful, in their colorful conjectures about the geology along the route.

The Topographic Corps was dispatched to survey the dynamic, unfamiliar landscape of the West and translate it into a practical technological foothold capable of fostering new forms of movement across a little-understood terrain. To quote William Goetzmann, "It was thus as a complex institution having a political, a military, a scientific and even a Romantic significance that the Corps of Topographical Engineers entered the West...self-consciously carrying the burden of civilization to the wilderness and the lessons of the wilderness back into civilization."[6] It is this dichotomy of interests between science and politics, documentation and imagination, discovery and communication that provides a fascinating platform from which to view the drawings in the Corps' reports and surveys.

While ultimately the explorations were inconclusive regarding the question of which railroad route to pursue, the reports did establish a scientific vision of the American West through extensive and experimental visualizations. With their broad strokes and descriptive travelogues, the Corps' work in its reports and surveys revealed a commitment to science that was interpretive rather than precise. In their creative visualizations we see, as historian Susan Schulten observes, "a change not just in cartographic techniques, but in thinking: the shift toward graphical information was both a cause and a consequence of modernization."[7] By synthesizing the new sights from the inner continent in this way, the Topographic Corps set a new agenda for the American West based in scientific inquiry, ecological speculation, and landscape experimentation. The images contained within the reports and surveys demonstrate how the explorations were an excursion of imagination, rather than simply a survey of specifics, positioning the Corps as architects of speculative vision and scientific imagination.

The Corps' novel mix of sketches, maps, charts, elevations, geologic imaginings, and cartographic projections participated in forming a new and transformative image–through purpose, understanding, and knowledge–of the American West. Five representation types–cartographic projections, scenographic landscapes, biological illustrations, charts and tables, and ecological diagrams–can be found in the reports and surveys. These are discussed in turn below.

Cartographic Projections

Cartographic Projections include plans, sections, relief maps, and profile cuts that abstract and structure the landscape through two-dimensional orthographics. It is worth noting that the surveys synthesized several previous maps from different eras of exploration. Lieutenant Gouverneur Kemble Warren's "Map of the Territory of the United States from the Mississippi to the Pacific Ocean" was one of the first detailed maps of the region. This master map integrated the work of several previous excursions, beginning with the documents from Merriweather Lewis and William Clark, and downplaying the work of Aaron Arrowsmith, the English cartographer whose map of the American West was considered most reliable to that point. This reconciliation of conflicting information was significant in developing a fuller understanding of continental space. Yet, for all of Warren's attention to detail and accuracy, he "downplayed–even erased–Native American knowledge, even when his Anglo-American 'authorities' relied on it."[8] In 1802, the Hudson Bay Company asked Blackfoot Chief Ac ko mok ki to create a map of the Missouri Basin that provided details about mountains, rivers, ecologies, and settlements in the continental interior. Hudson Bay sent the information back to London where Arrowsmith translated the notes into his map without crediting Ac ko mok ki. When Warren acknowledged the authority of Arrowsmith's work decades later, unsurprisingly Ac ko mok ki's geographic contributions had been erased.[9]

Throughout the Topographic Corps' reports two different types of cartographic projections are used to describe the scale and detail of the entire Trans-Mississippi West: traditional plan-view maps, as well as section cuts through the landscape. Each of these drawing types offered distinct levels of detail and abstraction, with different techniques used depending on the scale and resolution of each territory described. For example, in the plan drawings of mountainous regions, the two-dimensional surface of the paper seems to host striking topographical levels that communicate more about the qualitative experience of the land, versus section cuts which show a measured abstraction of the landscape. These profile cuts use precise graphic formulas to depict elevation, with line-weight and different scales and orientation of text charting the route. In both examples, the cartographic drawings are exceptionally large—folding out to cascade over several library tables—or at least, the desk of a prominent senator. Because of their size, the maps are capable of hosting a conversation, with several people standing around them looking at the detail and information presented, while also granting an authoritarian overview for those who commissioned the surveys.

Scenographic Landscapes

Most of 147 lithographs in the report are also drawn from this imperial overview. The sweeping landscapes are depicted from an elevated position, far above the horizon, continuing the presentation of territory for the congressmen back in Washington. Being able to possess the entire scene from this imagined vantage point also points to the tension the Topographic Corps encountered between objectivity and expression. Goetzmann describes this well:

> There was a conflict for most of the artists between the desire to paint the country as realistically as possible and the desire to express the grandeur and sublimity the new domain presented. Most of the artists were stunned by the variety they saw...distances more immense and overpowering than any the artists had previously known.[10]

The part-scientific, part-literary approach to natural history was typical of the scientific traditions and experiments emerging from Europe during the 19th century. Heinrich Mollhausen, a German scientist who joined Lieutenant Amiel Weeks Whipple's expedition across the 35th parallel, arrived on recommendation from Alexander von Humboldt. Mollhausen's expansive drawings of the landscape are noteworthy for their attention to geology. In particular, the exposed geology of the American West provided an almost direct translation of the systemic stratifications used in Humboldt's work.

Biological Illustrations

Developed in tandem with the Smithsonian Institution, the plant, animal, and fossil drawings included in the reports reflect well-established methods of representing biological forms. Several scales are used within the one drawing, facilitating an understanding of part-to-whole relationships. The zoological

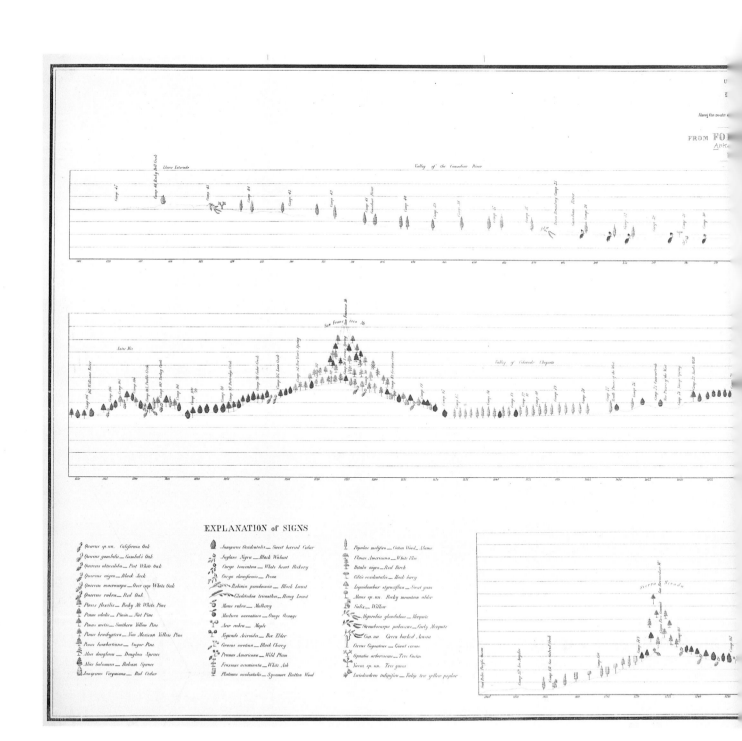

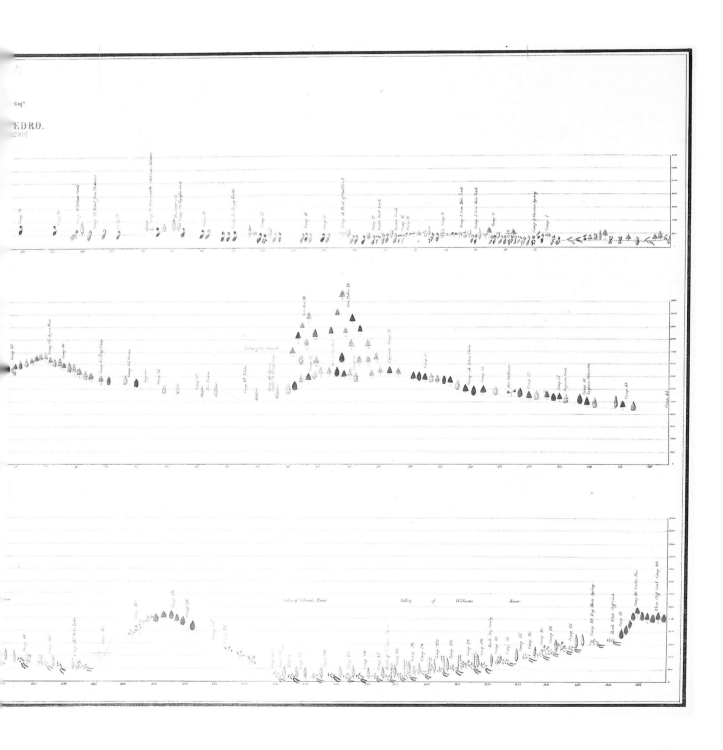

reports were separated into their own volumes, allowing detailed comparisons to be made between species collected along each route. Consolidating data between different surveying parties encouraged deeper cross referencing between the army and broader scientific community.

Charts and Tables

The Topographic Corps visualized their copious measurements through charts and tables, which one can consider as a scientific drawing due to the application of line weight, text alignment, and visual hierarchy that structures the data. Take, for example, two charts of precipitation and temperature. At first glance the two charts seem rather straightforward, even mundane, but three graphic techniques brilliantly structure their information. The first is text alignment: the months are all rotated in the top row to better align with numerical information below, specifically with the decimal point between all numbers, making for simple comparisons. Subtle indentations also structure the information, allowing data to be skimmed and quickly understood. Those alignments of information allow data to be grouped and nested together, creating tables within tables of information. Emphasizing those groupings is the strategic use of line weights between columns and rows, allowing information to be shaped by the heaviness of the line weights bracketing some information, or separated based on lighter line weights. The numerical data presented in the reports and surveys offers similar fluctuations in scale as seen in the previous drawing types.

Ecological Diagrams

Lastly, a new type of drawing emerged in the reports and surveys, which can best be described as "ecological diagrams." Highly illustrative, the drawings depict landscape dynamics and involve the charting, sectioning, and diagramming of dynamic processes, ecological relationships, and natural systems first studied by the Corps. While glimpses of these drawing types show up across the surveys, the work completed by the Whipple expedition, and including the team with the most direct relationship to Alexander von Humboldt, demonstrates a clear lineage and experimentation with this thinking.

Dr. Jules Marcou, a Swiss geologist and protégé of naturalist Louis Agassiz, joined the Whipple expedition on recommendation from Balduin Möllhausen. Marcou's geologic section cuts employ the bright colors and generalized shapes of contemporary architecture diagrams but are shaped and crafted using techniques of charting and organization. J.M. Bigelow, the expedition botanist, followed suit with a botanical diagram that combined information about tree specimens and elevation in the form of a section cut from the Mississippi to the Pacific. The drawings show icons hovering in space, giving a generalized information-graphic style of representation, yet are positioned in such a way that they respect lines of elevation and topography more commonly attributed to cartography. Techniques of simplification, profile cuts, vibrant colors, and strange layering of spaces describe a dynamic world, a highly fluctuating landscape, one that the stunned imagination needed to describe. These drawings, more so than the lithographs, demonstrate the type of landscape comprehension and speculation representative of the reports and surveys.

The diagrams also point to a significant and unidentified anxiety running through the Topographic Corps' work: how to overcome the challenge of attaching the brittle, heavy, fixed, iron and steel infrastructure required by the railroad onto an unpredictable, dynamic, erupting, shifting, and moving landscape? While the information gathered by the reports were significant for the scientific and military communities, the technological question of how to travel across the dynamic landscapes found in the American West fundamentally informs the majority of drawings. The speculative geological drawings, in particular, reveal layers of overlapping color and small icons and text floating mysteriously–unattached–over the landscape. Distant mountains appear as hovering figures, relieving themselves from a stabilizing ground plane. Isothermal maps point to the concerns about how wind and temperature would impact the railroad. The drawings in this section are highly speculative, utilizing a measured eye to express uncertainty and caution. While the work suggests a remarkable playfulness and lighthearted touch in describing novel landscape, the scale and scope of the work assembled grounds these less than purely scientific drawings into a military rigor familiar to the Army Corps of Engineers.

Though only active for a short period of time, the work of the Corps of Topographical Engineers through the *Railroad Reports* sets out a new scientific agenda by developing a visual language to comprehend nature. Novel forms of representation generated both a scientific and speculative imaginary of the American West. Not one or the other, but both. Data collection underpins speculation and imagination requires extrapolation. Between the scenographic and the scientific, the measured and the made up, the transition between comprehension and proposition, the *Railroad Reports* straddled politics and science while propelling emerging methods of scientific visualization and experimentation. Methods of layering collected data, topographic projection, and colorful landscape conjectures thus laid the groundwork for the era of post-Civil War surveys undertaken by the Department of the Interior, producing a vocabulary of graphic and visual information to propel a scientific imaginary.

1 The Army Corps of Engineers was officially established by Jefferson's Military Peace Establishment Act in 1802. It wasn't until 1863 that the Civil Engineering activities distributed across the military–cartography, land surveying, and public works construction–was synthesized under one organization.

2 D.W. Meining, *The Shaping of America: A Geographical Perspective on 500 Years of History. Volume 2: Continental America, 1800–1867* (Yale University Press, 1993), 3.

3 William H. Goetzmann, *Army Exploration in the American West*, 1803–1863 (Yale University Press, 1959), 262–63.

4 The significance of assembling so much intellectual power cannot be underscored enough. As Goetzmann describes, "Not since Napoleon had taken his company of savants into Egypt had the world seen such an assemblage of scientists and technicians marshaled under one banner. And like Napoleon's own learned corps, these scientists, too, were an implement of conquest, with the enemy in this case being the unknown reaches of the western continent."

5 Ibid., 308.

6 Ibid., 21.

7 Susan Schulten, *Mapping the Nation: History and Cartography in Nineteenth-Century America* (University of Chicago Press, 2012), 7.

8 Ibid., 53.

9 Ibid., 54.

10 Goetzmann, *Army Exploration in the American West*, 334.

CENTERING

THE FRINGE

JONAH SUSSKIND

Jonah Susskind is a senior research associate at SWA's XL Lab and a research coordinator at MIT's Norman B. Leventhal Center for Advanced Urbanism. His work has appeared in books and journals including *Design with Nature Now* (2019), *Wood Urbanism: From the Molecular to the Territorial* (2019), *Harvard Design Magazine*, and *JoLA*.

✛ REAL ESTATE, LAND PLANNING, CONSERVATION

Since the Gold Rush, California has been systematically urbanized through successive waves of speculative settlement, colonization, and peri-urban development. As the economic and ideological aspirations of a rapidly growing human population have collided with the physiographic complexities of the landscape itself, novel urban forms have proliferated along the outermost edges of metropolitan areas where the built environment comes into direct contact with surrounding ecosystems. These areas, officially known as the Wildland-Urban Interface (WUI), have spread rhizomatically through several decades of real estate speculation and leapfrog suburban expansion to become the fastest growing land use designation in the United States.[1] In California, the WUI is home to more than 11 million people – about one-quarter of the state's total population. By the turn of the next century, this number is expected to double.[2]

The WUI is a zone of constant conflict and negotiation between opposing worlds—both real and imagined—where the rigid Euclidean logics of land use planning and infrastructure meet the soft indeterminacy of existing natural landscape systems. In California, where the WUI overlaps with some of the world's most biodiverse and ecologically nuanced landscapes, this collision of human and nonhuman dynamics can be especially fraught.

For generations, California's market-driven approach to urbanization has transgressed against environmental common sense, catalyzing dangerous feedback loops between unchecked developer interests and increased exposure to environmental risks.[3] In a landscape that has been fundamentally shaped by a formidable list of natural hazards including perennial earthquakes, fires, floods, and mudslides, municipalities and other legislative bodies have done shockingly little to limit development of floodplains, seismic fault zones, and chronic wildfire corridors. As a result, stories of dangerous heat exposure, land subsidence, dry wells, and charred towns reveal the through lines that connect today's edge communities with the historical legacies of speculative development and the increasingly present manifestations of climate change.

During the past several years in particular, these collisions between human settlement and environmental hazards have become especially dramatic as rapid peri-urban growth has pushed deeper into California's most wildfire-prone landscapes. Record-breaking temperatures and extended dry seasons have coincided with a parallel increase in catastrophic conflagrations. Six of the state's 20 most destructive wildfires burned in 2020 alone, with associated costs eclipsing 12 billion dollars.[4] Experts caution that due to ongoing climate change the state has entered a new era of perennial megafires that will only become more destructive and more costly in the coming decades.

Much of this high-risk rural development has been driven by a severe statewide housing shortage. This scarcity has pushed low-income communities further from urban cores into unincorporated zones where land values and housing costs are less prohibitive, but where access to employment and social services is often scant. Since the start of the COVID-19 pandemic, these pressures have been compounded by fear of exposure and the rapid adoption of remote work scenarios, which have triggered yet another massive wave of exurban migration – bringing yet another generation of home-buyers into California's most precarious landscapes.[5]

Of course, today's cities don't end at their municipal boundaries. They leak out, seeping into adjacent watersheds, altering ecosystems, stretching deep into the most remote hinterlands to extract essential metabolic inputs, and dispersing themselves into the atmosphere through airborne particulate and greenhouse gas emissions. As California and the rest of the planet race to curtail the worst-case scenarios projected by climate scientists, the WUI finds itself at the convergence of ongoing debates about infrastructure, resource management, energy production, and regional resilience.

These transitional peri-urban zones represented by the WUI offer both a spatial and an intellectual platform for reflecting upon the contemporary urban experience for an increasingly comprehensive cross-section of the US population. Most of those moving to cities today are not doing so to inhabit their cores, but rather to compete for space along their sprawling margins.[6] Yet, these areas of settlement and the landscapes they are situated within continue to proliferate with shockingly little input or consideration from the design community. This conspicuous lack of engagement reflects the degree to which urbanization has become understood as "cityization," rather than as an ongoing process of regional interconnectivity, structured and fueled by both city and non-city spaces and their associated communities.[7]

The WUI represents a disciplinary challenge for urbanists because it embodies an erosion of formal legibility. It evades typological standardization and is governed by an asymmetrical assortment of regulatory frameworks and land use classifications. Yet, radical and irreversible transformations are taking place in these vast fringe zones at rates commensurate with the pace of population growth and economic development in today's urban cores.[8]

It is in this context that active engagement with the WUI offers sweeping opportunities for critical disciplinary reflection and creative speculation that move beyond a preoccupation with the city as the essential urban form. By expanding the urban imaginary to include these lower-density morphological expressions of fringe-ness, we can begin to understand how the vibrant nexus of socio-spatial relationships between geographies of capitalism and the landscape itself continues to drive 21st-century processes of metropolitan settlement.

1 Sebastián Martinuzzi, et al., "The 2010 Wil land Urban Interface of the Conterminous United States" (US Department of Agriculture, Forest Service, Northern Research Station, 2015].

2 Michael L. Mann, et al., "Modeling Residential Development in California from 2000 to 2050: Integrating Wildfire Risk, Wildland and Agricultural Encroachment," *Land Use Policy* 41 (November 1, 2014]: 438–52.

3 Mike Davis, "How Eden Lost Its Garden," in *Ecology of Fear: Los Angeles and the Imagination of Disaster* [Metropolitan Books, 1998], ch. 2.

4 Geographic Area Coordination Center, "2020 National Large Incident Year to Date Report" (National Interagency Fire Center, 2020].

5 Laura Bliss & Marie Patino, "Where Americans Moved Into Fire Danger Zones," *Bloomberg.Com*, https://www.bloomberg.com/graphics/2021-moves into fire zones/ (accessed November 20, 2021].

6 Shlomo Ange,l et al., "Densify and Expand: A Global Analysis of Recent Urban Growth," *Sustainability* 13, no. 7 (January 2021]: 3835.

7 Neil J. Brenner [ed.], *Implosions/Explosions: Towards a Study of Planetary Urbanization* [Jovis, 2014].

8 Shlomo Angel, et al., "Engaging with the Planet's Urban Expansion," in Alan Berger, Joel Kotkin & Celina Balderas Guzmán [eds], *Infinite Suburbia* [Princeton Architectural Press, 2017], 164–77.

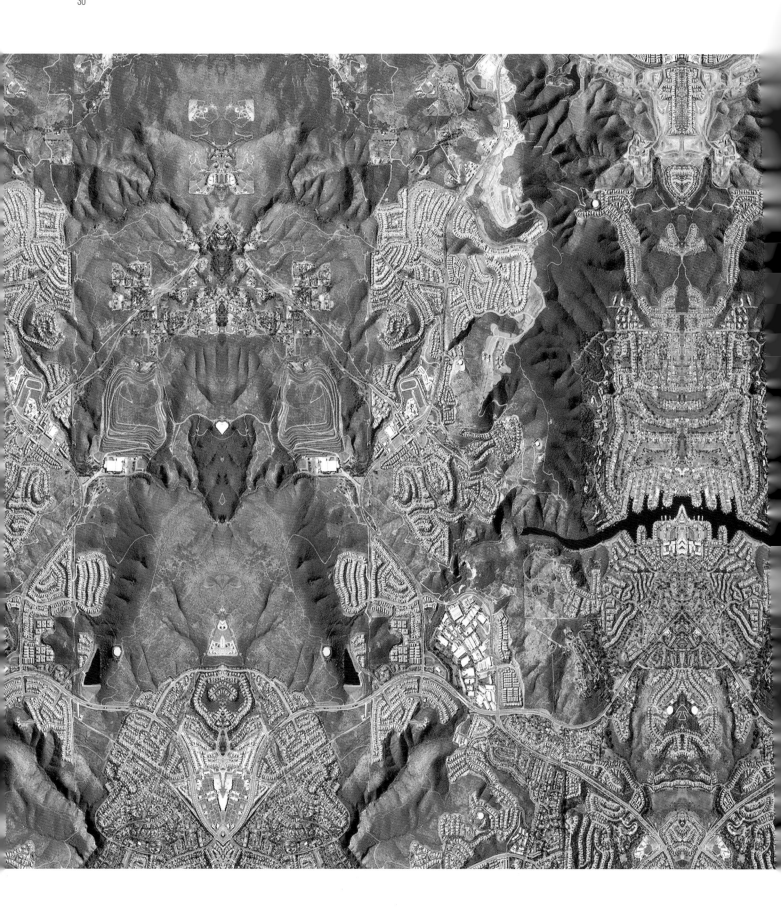

Opposite: Escondido Rock Summit.
Above: Speculative Settlement Composite,
Northern California.

Opposite: Kettleman Valley Crossing.
Above: Speculative Settlement Composite,
Central California.

Opposite: Frontier Lake Trails.
Above: Speculative Settlement Composite,
Southern California.

THE PLANE TABLE
A TOOL OF SPECULATION

ADRIAN HAWKER

Adrian Hawker is a senior lecturer in architectural design (contemporary practices) at the Edinburgh School of Architecture and Landscape Architecture (ESALA) and program director of the Master of Architecture at the University of Edinburgh. He is founder and codirector (with Mark Dorrian) of Metis, an atelier for art, architecture, and urbanism. Hawker's theoretical design work has been awarded, exhibited, and published internationally.

+ ARCHITECTURE, CARTOGRAPHY

Within the digital photographic archive of the US Coast and Geodetic Survey[1]–the agency established in 1807 by Thomas Jefferson under the title of "Survey of the Coast"–is a striking image that depicts two men carefully balanced upon a boulder that rises from a wide body of water. The image title informs us that they are part of the crew of the survey vessel *The Explorer*, which was commissioned in 1921 to map the south-eastern coast of Alaska. The man on the left of the image is crouched, poised in action and focused intently on something in the distance, far beyond the frame of the image. By way of contrast, the man on the right holds a more restful, casual stance – one that seeks to maintain comfort in stillness. His gaze is on the first man, and he is clearly there to assist his work. Between them, straddling this miniature island, is a tripod of outstretched crutch-like timber limbs that supports, at chest level, a white horizontal plane. Upon the surface of this plane projects a prop that further positions, at eye level, an optical tool. And it is through the lens of this device that the first man's vision is held. Two forms of shelter complete this composition: an umbrella is held by the second man to shelter the actions of the first and, at his feet, is a case seemingly scaled to hold the white datum and its disassembled scope. The leather strap attached to the case suggests that this was recently fastened to his back as he and his companion journeyed to this most unlikely of destinations.

The surveying device with which they are engaged is a plane table and the black and white photograph is one of a number cataloged in the Plane Table Mapping section of the National Oceanic and Atmospheric Administration's "Topography – Mapping the Shoreline" collection.[2] Each photograph depicts a comparable, often unintentionally comical, balancing act performed through the precarious negotiations of an equivalent device with a liminal world that is neither fully land nor water.

We see them balanced upon similar rocks or on the ragged undercut forms of coral islets. Some are held within the branches of overhanging trees or on the dormant metallic wings of seaplanes. Others stand on the unsure ground of tidal sand or temporal sheets of glacial ice. We see some chest deep in water while others are caught within the fecundity of mangroves. No matter the extremity of context, the basic composition is the same – a surveyor hunched over a white surface, a pencil in one hand and the other focusing the lens of a viewfinder.

Below the horizontal plane is suspended a roll that suggests a length of paper that can be drawn across the white surface to form a greater set of graphic notations. The paper is presumably extended with each delicate iteration of the tripod. In so doing, a drawn manuscript map would slowly emerge, developed through the continuous engagement of a metal ruler affixed to, and therefore choreographed by, the viewfinder. This combination of sight and rule forms an alidade that can be turned to line up with a position of interest, allowing a pencil line to then be drawn along its straight edge to describe an axis between viewer and this feature. The alidade can be used with other, more conventional, drawing implements such as scales, compasses, and a setsquare. Through their joint engagement, a form of elongated cartographic manuscript slowly materializes, one that depicts first-hand the landscape negotiated by both surveyors and tripod.

The plane table lacks the precision of the theodolite, which undertakes a survey through an entirely numerical form of measurement. This empirical abstraction differentiates it from the graphic directness of the plane table. A survey developed through a plane table forms the first draft of a map in the field. It evolves through a close engagement with a process of drawing.

A survey undertaken with the use of a theodolite delays such graphic interpretation until the recordings have been returned safely to the drawing office, whereas a map developed upon the surface of a plane table emerges *live* during the moment of observation. It bypasses many of the requirements of measurement and, instead, relies more directly, more bodily, on looking and drawing as a performative act where something is considered and represented through the speculative process of observation itself.

The plane table enables a mapping to take place in the context of the very territory under scrutiny. The contiguity of this process not only requires the employment of a pre-planned strategy but also a fair degree of intuition. While it is a carefully structured procedure, survey points are not necessarily all predetermined. Many, if not most, are identified, revealed, through the act of drawing itself. Relationships, connections, observations, and discoveries are literally *drawn out* through the procedural development of the manuscript map. Inevitably, this process is open to distraction.

Cartographers engaging with a plane table operate beyond the secure environment of the drafting room. They have to be agile, able to respond to the unexpected, to instances of change and shifting emphasis. They draw and create while being exposed to the full sensorial experience of the landscape of their inquiry – its sounds, quality of light, weather, wind direction, and surrounding social activity. The ground they depict is not empty, it is occupied – time passes there. Life takes place upon the land and its events and biographies are caught within the unfolding net of survey lines. The field of operation is not solely defined by physical terrain but is also revealed to be a *field of influences* – observed moments drawn from the landscape. With the aid of the umbrella and the

tripod, tiny, temporary drafting rooms are peppered across the landscape. Each one seeking out and establishing the perfect site for speculation before being enfolded back into the case and moving on. For the cartographers in Alaska, each time their plane table was employed, a nascent map was unfurled just a few feet above the very landscape that was being both observed and experienced.

For a number of years, I have been engaged in a teaching practice with the artist Victoria Clare Bernie within the Edinburgh School of Architecture and Landscape Architecture (ESALA) which is part of both the Edinburgh College of Art and the University of Edinburgh. Together, we have been running a series of one- and two-year post graduate studio programs under the banner of "Island Territories." We have mainly been working with Master of Architecture students but also, on occasion, with those in the Master of Landscape Architecture program. Our interest in islands stems from their fascinating and frequently strange propensity to condense and embody themes and issues pertaining to the political, social, economic, and ecological environment. Equally, we are intrigued by their tendency to nurture a culture that is able blur the harsh realities of isolation with the marvelous narratives of identity. Repeatedly, these themes revel themselves through the acute relationship between the historic island settlement and the limitations and mineral value of the landscape upon which they were founded. Within these studios, our initial moves have encouraged the development of inventive and complex forms of representational constructs that are charged with analyzing, drawing out, and speculating upon the rich potentials of this relationship.

These representational devices are ambitious, collaborative acts that engage material fabrication alongside the conventions of drawing. Their ardent materiality and craft enable a subtle blurring between their role as analytical tools that measure and re-present a landscape, and their performance as a material, tectonic, and spatial prompt that can be offered back to these contexts as a speculative proposition. As a consequence, the thesis projects that have emerged from such work tend to be steeped with the material and graphic narratives of the multivalent landscape of their particular island territory. In recent years, we have come to see these constructs and drawings as being analogous to the device of the plane table. They are tools that act out and directly inscribe into their surfaces the act of discovery and analysis in the moment it takes place. Like the plane table, they are initially established on the unsure ground of the unfamiliar. They seek to find their position among a sea of information. However, as particular points of reference become established, a focused and speculative strategy emerges that allows students to form connections between seemingly remote sightings.

The photograph from Alaska mentioned above portrays an act of one island being established upon another island: one real, the miniature island of the boulder beneath; and one representational, the graphic drawing and its apparatus above. Both are exposed to the environment around them. The boulder is gnarled and cracked by the freezing and thawing of the water and pitted and encrusted by the temporality of the shifting tides and the sea life carried within. Despite the rudimentary protection of the umbrella and the case, within its own vastly compressed timeframe, the manuscript map becomes stained, tainted, and weathered by repeated exposure and persistent movement. The plane table also absorbs peripheral information. Within the marginalia of the field notes of John Randel Jr on his epic survey to lay the grid of Manhattan are his observations on flora and fauna and, on occasion, such intimate incidents as a recipe gleaned from a local farmworker or the tentative draft of a letter to his wife back home.[3] The later entries to the journals of Colonel William Light, the founding surveyor of the South Australian city of Adelaide, are obsessed with the weather, the dark brooding clouds seemingly reflecting Light's emotional state of prolonged homesickness.[4] Work in the field is clearly prone to distraction.

These analogous plane tables have encouraged our students to embrace distraction and to understand it as part of the true context of a place. Rather than seeing them operate solely within the empirical world of data collection–a reductive process that seeks safety in numbers and a world all to easily consumed by a diagram–we have enjoyed the complexities of layering and the interaction of thematic concerns. Things get caught in the grain of such works - names and their meanings, biographies and quotations, flora, fauna and, indeed, more weather. *Scoring the Malecón* (2018, previous page),[5] a construct of timber, plaster, brass, glass, and steel by four ESALA students–Alecsandra Trofin, Sheryl Lam, Ezmira Peraj, and Leo Xian–was fabricated as precursor to their joint "Malecón Sea Room" thesis proposal for Havana. It unpacked the narratives of the sea-drenched and hurricane-beaten terraced apartments of Havana's famous seawall esplanade and inscribed them onto a speculative surface of oak. These stories, meticulously collected through first-hand interviews with the ageing occupants, were encouraged to interact among data pertaining to the city's revolutionary history and the environmental crisis this city edge now endures.

The plane table may lack the exactitude of the empirical survey but sometimes this is appropriate. The ruinous no-man's land of Nicosia's Green Line–the UN patrolled buffer zone that has cloven the Cypriot capital into the Turkish occupied north and the Greek Orthodox south since the Turkish invasion of Cyprus in 1974–is all too readily depicted on maps as hard edged, precise, and specific. The reality on the ground is less clearly defined. The physical border exists somewhere between sporadic signage, the crumbling ruins of buildings, chaotic layers of wire, and dense, sprawling vegetation. It is not uncommon for a house backed up against this zone to take the opportunity to propagate a garden from a patch of its land or for discarded materials within the zone to be harvested and utilized in unofficial construction on its periphery. ESALA students Chiara Fingland and Sarah Comfort's drawing and associated constructs of the *Diachronic Garden* (2016, opposite) sought to further examine this observation and depict the edge as a loose, thickened condition and, in so doing, speculated on strategies for the vacant zone's future inhabitation and cultivation – a process of "seeding in" from this thickened edge.

A table, by its nature, is a place of exchange and collaboration: people gather around it and share. The survey operatives in Alaska face each other across a table. One supports the other, they share the extraordinary experience of this landscape and the arduous act of traversing it. We have found in our studios that the conceptual frame of the plane table has encouraged students to collaborate in a variety of ways. From the shared work of information gathering and fabrication, to the discursive speculations that operate within and well beyond the temporal confines of the formal tutorial. Ideas are "tabled," put forward, rearranged, collected, stored, and temporarily forgotten – only to re-emerge later as a prompt for an unexpected move. Games are played out on tables and speculations are tested. These interactions may be wholly collaborative, producing a single work with one voice, or constantly negotiated – the table as a common site or field upon which separate projects speak.

The *Klaksvík Table* (2014) by Oliver Bywater, Kris Gratz, and Emily Nason is a case in point. Three separate concerns, embodied through a "chair" construct, were pulled up to a table initially inscribed with the bathometric soundings of the deep fjord of Klaksvík that cuts into Borðoy, an island in the northeast Faroe archipelago. As the Faroes township gathers around the shared concern of this body of water, so did these speculative tools. Each then acted out their independent scenarios through a form of continuous conversation and interplay. The surface of the table, like that of a dinner party, recorded the choreography of this dialogue as a trace of a speculative performance.

The *Lagoon Atlas* (2012) by Laura Barr and Emma Garland took the notion of a glass worker's bench as a starting point for a speculative mapping of the Fondamenta Nove, the 16th-century promenade that sealed the northeastern edge of the Venetian *sestiere* of Cannaregio. Through a considered reflection on the process of glassmaking—from the dredging and sifting of Lagoon sands to the firing of kilns in the historic workshops of the nearby cluster of islands that form Murano—a table of sorts was devised to record an imagined journey from Cannaregio to these islands of glassmakers. The surface of the table was modulated to act as a filter where dredged material could be placed, examined, and sorted into a system of embedded trays to form a taxonomy of the lagoon floor. Two people could meet on either side of the table and lift its surface to reveal an atlas of the changing optical field of the journey from either port. The table was thus conceived to be set and "read" at the midpoint between the two. The atlas revealed the resultant frayed nature of the sightlines, disturbed by the extraordinary architectural constructs of the islands and their adjacencies. Such a fraying was appropriate to Venice—a city that bleeds into water—and thereby brought into question the harsh rigidity of the failed project of the Fondamenta Nove.

Sanctuary for Suspended States (2020)[6] by Lauren Copping, Grace Losasso, and Jessica Thomson was initially conceived as a balancing act, taking precedent from Philippe Petit who famously walked a tightrope between the twin towers of the World Trade Center in New York City on the morning of August 7, 1974. In his studio, Petit practiced on what he termed "the smallest theater in the world," a stage no larger than a table. The measurements of this defined the scale of the students' construct to which detailed maps of the area around Manhattan's historic Collect Pond were enlarged. Through a form of inverse archaeology, the history of this area from the present-day judicial field of law courts and prisons to the natural spring-fed reservoir that bled through meadows and salt marshes to the Hudson, was enacted as an aerial suspension – each piece counterbalanced by another. This peeling away of layers inspired the students to speculate on a future for this area where the capping of the earth through the current array of heavy plinths and courtyards was replaced by a lighter layering of inhabited decks and water channels with water once again engaged to choreograph movement and program.

In many ways, each of these works has operated as a form of plane table in reverse. In the field, the plane table is constantly identifying points of reference and absorbing them into the act of drawing. In our studios, the plane tables, having absorbed archival cartographies, observations, and analysis create a field of references around them. This is a representational context, but one that is also highly visceral and experiential. In the photograph of the surveyors in Alaska, the limited rocky ground on which they precariously work is vivid and detailed in its description, but the landscape beyond is vague and elusive. The rippled surface of the water extends to white, merging with the sky. The coastal edge, the primary subject of the surveyor's concern, begins and then fades into this point of merger. They are slowly defining the context around them. With each positioning of the table, each tripod adjustment, each surface levelling, each focus of the sight, and each inscription of line, the context becomes more tangible, more real. The plane table draws out the world through a process of performative engagement.

And so, too, do the student works presented here. The worlds they describe are real in that they are informed by the discipline of measured, carefully researched analysis and observation. But they are also, using the term of the Cuban writer (and cultural surveyor of his own island), Alejo Carpentier, *marvelous* in that they intuit future possibilities – *speculations* imagined through their spatial materiality and the manner and invention evident in their construction. Richard Sennet articulates this beautifully in his essay "Arousing Tools" published in his book *The Craftsman:*

> Without detracting from the experience, I have sought to take some of the mystery out of intuition. It can be crafted. Tools used in certain ways organize this imaginative experience and with productive results. Both limited and all-purpose instruments can enable us to take the imaginative leap necessary to repair material reality or guide us towards what we sense is an unknown reality latent with possibility.[7]

The plane table is, indeed, such a tool. One that crafts intuition and guides speculation.

1 National Geodetic Survey, US Coast and Geodetic Survey: https://www.ngs.noaa.gov/web/about_ngs/history/.

2 National Oceanic and Atmospheric Administration Photo Library, "Topography – Mapping the Shoreline" collection, *Plane Table Mapping*, https://www.photolib.noaa.gov/Collections/Coast-Geodetic-Survey/Geodesy/Topography-Mapping-the-Shoreline/Plane-Table-Mapping.

3 Marguerite Hollaway, *The Measure of Manhattan: The Tumultuous Career and Surprising Legacy of John Randel Jr. Cartographer, Surveyor, Inventor* (W.W. Norton & Company, 2013).

4 Paul Carter, "Light Reading," in *The Lie of the Land* (Faber & Faber Ltd, 1996).

5 See Adrian Hawker & Victoria Clare Bernie, Island Territories V: Havana, *Re-making Islands, Dismantling Insularity* (ESALA, University of Edinburgh, 2018), https://issuu.com/eca.march/docs/2017-18_havana.

6 See Adrian Hawker & Victoria Clare Bernie, *Island Territories VI: Manhattan Scapeland* (ESALA, University of Edinburgh, vol. 1, 2019) https://issuu.com/eca.march/docs/2018-19_manhattan and vol. 2 (2020) https://issuu.com/eca.march/docs/2019-20_manhattan.

7 Richard Sennett, *The Craftsman* (Allen Lane, 2008), 213.

STUART CANDY + AROUSSIAK GABRIELIAN

FUTURING:
A CONVERSATION

The discipline of landscape architecture often speaks of its unique capacity for engaging with considerations of time, be it unearthing the lost histories of a site, elevating the concerns of a culture, or embracing the tangible transformation of materials—particularly living materials—over time. Yet one thing with which the discipline is rarely associated is the future - at least in terms of projecting possibilities or offering unfamiliar realities. The principal material media of the landscape discipline are not often understood in terms of innovation or technological novelty, but rather are associated with authenticity, natural systems, and embedded culture. Within the public imagination, invention in landscape is hidden behind seemingly familiar images of the natural.

On the other hand, futuring—or future studies, foresight thinking, or scenario design among its many other descriptions—is concerned, as the name implies, solely with possibilities beyond today. As a method of inquiry, futuring plays out plausible situations and circumstances that might emerge from weak signals, strengthening trends, or new data. It concerns itself both with what is and what is not desired. Notably, however, it is rarely spatial in its elaboration, instead manifesting its work in the form of white papers, workshops, and what-ifs. Futuring is not in the business of predicting, but rather provoking reflection.

Yet despite these seemingly divergent concerns, there is a great deal of potential in the notion of futuring landscape—that is, in the rigorous consideration of landscape futures—both as a method of practice and a form of engagement. This is particularly true as it relates to concerns around climate change and the recentering of culture. In the conversation that follows, Stuart Candy—associate professor in the Carnegie Mellon School of Design and an award-winning foresight practitioner—talks with Aroussiak Gabrielian—a transdisciplinary practitioner working across the fields of landscape architecture and media arts—about the possibilities and potentials of intersecting landscape concerns and capacities with the methodologies and possibilities of futuring.

Stuart Candy So, we're meeting for the first time, which is an exciting chance to bring ideas together! You were saying that the encounter between futures studies and landscape architecture has barely begun. Tell me more.

Aroussiak Gabrielian I think an encounter between the fields of landscape architecture and futures studies has not yet entered pedagogy or practice in any systematic, structured, or serious way. Yet, there is a lot of affinity between the two fields that I think could provide productive ground for conversation, particularly as it relates to the climate crisis and social and environmental justice.

Landscape architecture is fundamentally a temporal discipline. It works with ecologies that shift and change over time, it negotiates a multiplicity of timescales – geologic, biologic, and cultural. And so, this engagement with temporality–or thinking through time–is already embedded in and very much part of the core of the discipline. However, I think in practice, and at times in pedagogy, landscape architecture often gets trapped in the methodological limits that it has inherited from

the engineering fields – whereby it identifies a problem to be solved, and then pursues, or is driven by finding solutions to, the problem. It therefore forgets, at times, to question the actual structures and systems that might have put that problem on the ground in the first place. While the solutions might be designed with the long term in mind, the approach is actually a kind of short-term thinking. And I think one area that the futures field can help push landscape architecture toward, is to break free or avoid these solutionist methodologies by borrowing, instead, methods used in futures studies that give landscape architects the permission to engage with a less deterministic idea of the future and a longer time horizon in our work.

Methods that you've been developing with Jeff Watson, and also in your own work with performance, provide helpful pathways to get us to snap out of the bounds or limits of thinking in the short term. You're trained to understand these kinds of big, governing systems through patterns and are somehow able to engage more freely with alternatives, at least more freely than we are trained to do. The multiplicity and plurality of possibilities that you move toward is both fascinating and relevant, and, I would say, desperately needed in the field of landscape architecture to help bring about more transformative change.

So that realization happened during my PhD studies, when I was studying with Jeff and working with Alex McDowell in the Worldbuilding Media Lab at the School of Cinematic Arts at USC. I was building out my PhD work, which is

speculative in nature, and both Jeff and Alex were exposing me to all these thinkers in the futures field, as well as to methods that might help build a kind of scaffold for the work that I was engaging in. Among that material was your dissertation and the game that you and Jeff codesigned, as well as the other methods that Alex worked with in his lab. Prior to the exposure to these methodologies, I had felt like speculation was perhaps more of an experiment in imagination, and what I've realized is that there is a structured framework that guides this kind of work. And I think that was really interesting and useful to understand: that this was something that could be taught, reproduced, and applied in different situations and contexts.

SC What are ways in which landscape architecture is maybe coming up short, in view of the types of challenges you've alluded to?

AG Too often landscape architectural practice relies on problem-solution frameworks for physical fixes to the multi-scalar and multi-dimensional challenges we are facing as a species, as a society, and as a planet. So, for instance, what I have my students do is not only propose designs, but also the kind of mechanisms that might allow for certain kinds of systemic change to take shape. I tend to have my students start with a landscape system instead of a site. And I ask them to discover the site of their intervention through a close study of those systems.

SC So, the modes of speculation involved in that kind of work, what do they look like? How does the thinking about future states manifest?

AG Well, it's definitely a difficult task for students because even after they land in their sites, they often forget all the research that got them there and revert back to what feels more comfortable to them as a working method: solving problems. And some of the methods I have them work through to overcome this utilizes the tools used in the future field: engaging in gameplay and performance, like the game you and Jeff invented.

SC Oh, you mean *The Thing from The Future?*

AG Yes! And when students have to really consider these various different timescales that the game pushes them to think about, be it 10 years from now or 100 years from now, and the four future scenarios that might define their topic, it helps them rethink their initial instincts. And it was from practicing with these methods in both my doctoral studies and in the classroom that I thought, there's so much usefulness in these for our field to work with. From my work with Jeff and Alex, I've probably been exposed to, I don't know, four or five different methods, but I'm sure there are many others that could potentially prove to be productive for landscape architects.

SC That's interesting. I was having a conversation yesterday at the Berggruen Institute in our working group on creative futures. My colleague Johanna Hoffman ran a super stimulating workshop that used a kind of live action roleplaying approach, imagining ourselves in the year 2045, in a hypothetical megacity similar to Los Angeles or São Paulo, with a complex layered mixture of elements both real and imaginary to respond to. In the debrief afterwards, what came to mind was something that the jazz musician Charles Mingus once said: "You can't improvise on nothing."

Whenever you're trying to imagine any future, even if you don't provide any deliberate prompts, people's brains are still bound to find something to think with – their assumptions, their experiences, or perhaps the sci-fi movies or books that happen to be called up by whatever the theme might be. But it's also possible to set ourselves up to try to respond to too many things at once, like trying to improvise in multiple keys or time signatures simultaneously. And so there are some practical psychological limitations to account for. This recognition is also a point of departure for the framework of a creative prompt-based game like *The Thing from The Future*: the idea is, let's use these particular, finite ingredients to both constrain and enable imaginative responses. People have a lot of capabilities, but we're also limited. We need to find ways to make these tasks manageable for ourselves.

AG So how did you bring design into the futures field? How did that happen for you?

SC By the time I got to grad school, I'd worked for the Australian and British governments on wonky white paper-type research with a futures bent, but largely expressed in words, statistics, and charts. These types of projects are very responsible, playing it straight, but in the process almost kneecapping ourselves by not doing anything very visual or embodied, or even memorable, let alone inspiring. I have a history in theater, and so while studying futures in grad school, at the University of Hawaii at Manoa, my colleague Jake Dunagan and I found ourselves asking: what if we physically immersed people into the scenarios we wanted them to discuss? What if we put charismatic pieces of those futures in their hands? What if we took these worlds of tomorrow and overlaid them on the world of today, in places where people live and work? If these ideas about the future could be made to land in the gut, and in the heart, then they might have a shot at actually being remembered, at changing behavior, at infiltrating institutions and public life.

And after I started blogging about this stuff in 2006, I soon came across people in other fields, especially design, who, as I saw it, were groping their way toward the same intersection but coming from the other direction. These fellow travelers, people like Julian Bleecker, or Tony Dunne and Fiona Raby, and some of their protégés, were using their design tools and training in service of exploring bigger picture, more far-reaching, more imaginative vistas. And perhaps a reason why design futures, design fiction, and speculative design have exploded in the way that they have over the last 10 years or so is because the desire of people–particularly students, and there's a generational factor here too, I think–to do something meaningful, addressing the planetary predicament in its many dimensions is given a much-needed outlet by the embrace of the right to speculate.

AG I'm wondering how you feel about the pitfalls in speculative design, given the criticism it has received for being speculation for speculation's sake or that its focus has been very techno-scientific, or product driven – pushing forth the same capitalist system by inventing objects that we might consume in the future.

SC Yeah, I think that those are definitely ways the work can fail to live up to its potential. Sometimes, especially early on, practitioners might find themselves using an excess of whimsy on one hand, or an excess of capitalist realism on the other. To me, both are ways of missing the mark, but I think it would be unfortunate if that were to lead some observers to think that the whole enterprise of using design and the arts to explore futures is without value. That would be a grand-scale throwing out of the baby with the bathwater. It's possible to write bad poetry, too, but that doesn't mean all poetry is bad.

I would say that some of the criticism drawn during the recent wave of speculation in design, while fair enough, is really responding to a sort of belated unleashing of creative energy that was previously stifled by a so-called human centered, but, let's be honest, capital-centered, paradigm where the use of imagination is highly constrained, and aspirational only within tightly defined limits. You take those constraints off, and people go wild. That is actually kind of cool to watch, but is it the end state for the practice? I don't think so. Once people have gotten some of that initial rambunctious energy out of their system, there is a sort of getting of wisdom in play. You can see this with The Thing from The Future. To start with, many players revel in the license to run free, be silly, and have fun. Then, after a while, they start to get a little bit more critical and search for ideas with more substance. The novelty of the very idea of something ostensibly coming "from the future," perhaps exciting enough in itself to begin with, wears off, and players start to want to know more about what future it's from, and how it might work, and how it's different from what they've heard before, and whose interests it represents. This is part of why, having created the game, Jeff and I kept adapting and modifying it, and using it with different groups to help push the general vogue for speculation past this initial flare-up of excitement and crappy ideas that we all tend to have when first invited to roam freely in the space of alternative futures.

To try to make the year 2050 matter right now is an important but difficult task. There's no objective referent for a 2050 scenario – in contrast to trying to bridge into the shoes of someone historically or in the present, where you can at least partially ground-truth things. The inbuilt speculative challenge of futures is that they are not just epistemically but ontologically indeterminate. They are up for grabs. So we need to realize that when we're making a hypothetical world specific enough to wrap our body-minds around, we're making it artificially specific, just in order to be able to think and feel into it. We have to take the ability to inhabit this "what if" with a big grain of salt, because it's not a question of getting it right or not, in a predictive sense; it's a question of how rigorously and usefully we are deploying imagination to enable new perceptions and possibilities in the present.

AG There's a similarity here to how some landscape designers work with the past and the present, which is interesting. Some literally excavate the ground for hints of things that once existed that they try to bring to the surface. So designing with history in some cases ends up being really tangible. And designing in the present often involves engaging communities on the ground and incorporating their voice into projects. But, that long-term horizon is the hardest for students to grapple with. Because, again, in that circumstance they don't have anything tangible to hold on to.

Now I don't know if you have an answer to this, but one thing that I notice about the futures field is that it seems to be very human centric. When it comes to the nonhuman, how do you grapple with such systems that also need to be heard and brought to the foreground?

SC Yes; there's been–especially among our design PhD and master's students–a surge of interest in the, perhaps quixotic, but very important, effort to take the perspective of other species, entities, or actors. And I've also been thinking recently about how future governance might incorporate the voices of nonhuman species, a generation or two.

For example, an experiential futures project that we did last year for the United Nations Development Programme included a hypothetical artifact, physically delivered to the home address of Sophie Howe, the Welsh Commissioner for Future Generations – a real person, and a real job! But the gift that she received from the future was a

government mailout from the Parliament of All Beings, which in the year 2056 is overseeing an urban rewilding project in her neighborhood in Cardiff, where other species have a say in whether and when humans are allowed back in.

Governance is a set of mechanisms that we have for collectively shaping things, and designing for the futures of governance requires a somewhat "meta" move, trying to picture what the system could look like if it were arranged to produce the preferred futures that we would like to see. Following these threads can lead to envisioning a world where governments and organizations are set up very differently, and take different voices into account. We can never fully escape the fact of our embodiment and our anthropocentrism, but I think we can make more space for challenges to them.

AG Yes! It's a similar dilemma in design as well. One of the ways I've tried to work with nonhuman species is by actually trying to collaborate with other organisms to bring their agency into the work itself. But I realize that time has gotten away from us, and before we round off our conversation I wanted to ask you: there's a whole lineage of backcasting in your field that arrives at preferred futures and then designs the means to get us there. And part of it is possibly through policy, as you described, but there's potentially other methods. Have you been involved in projects that are in the process of arriving at the kinds of futures that you've envisioned or what might that process look like? What are the different forms it takes?

SC That's a hell of a curly question to end on!

AG I know; but it's the promise of those alternative models for our field and beyond that I'm drawn to. How we can slowly move beyond the feeling of being trapped in someone else's imagination and ultimately arrive at more relational or ethical models of existence. I see these methods as both a form of resistance and as an agent of change that imagines a way out of the prison of our deeply troubling present.

SC We have to think about where to intervene in terms of multiple levels, as Donella Meadows suggested. If we're talking about discourse, or society's conversation about itself, as a system, there's a kind of Gregory Bateson idea here too, of a mental ecology; the things that we think about and don't think about being not just the product of the workings of our minds, but co-constructed by the environments we move through. I think it's reasonable to see ourselves as intervening simultaneously on an ambient level as well as in particular situations – classrooms, conferences, strategic conversations, policy, or election processes, and so on. Not every project needs to lead in a straight line to "and this resulted in this impact." We can consider the exercise of cultural influence in this more diffuse way, like a slow-release drug into the water supply, as my former Arup colleague Dan Hill has put it.

On that level, it seems to me that we have made some real headway in recent years, as a community of practitioners. Various "discursive design" strategies are now standard in the repertoire of the design worlds you and I are in, but beyond that too, in the cultural sector.

Many major museums have done exhibitions of future artifacts, and there are whole new institutions like the Museum of Tomorrow in Rio or the Museum of the Future in Dubai. The Smithsonian has an exhibition open right now on the National Mall in DC, called The Futures. Looking further afield, to other spaces, at the International Federation of Red Cross and Red Crescent Societies we used design and experiential futures interventions that helped launch an extraordinarily rapid uptake of futures thinking in the humanitarian sector. Many other organizational and policy contexts are picking up on these approaches as well.

I guess more diffuse shifts in practices and values may be hard to nail down, in terms of which actions produced which impacts, but I'm okay with that, because to me these are all essential steps toward a distributed, society-wide "social foresight" capacity. And in any case, the drive to linear evaluation is part of a bean-counting culture that I don't believe to be as legitimate as it thinks it is! I don't know, did that answer your question?

SC To close, do you have any thoughts about where the confluence of futures and landscape design might lead, or where we should be nudging it, if we're agents in this?

AG Well, I think there are some rich areas of overlap where I see the two almost speaking the same language, or at least nurturing the same desire. And yet as disciplines, each one also has its own flavor. I think we should initiate more conversations and collaborations, to start.

SC Yeah, and this is a good start! Just to touch on one of those overlaps: because it's very difficult to talk about time directly, we end up discussing futures in terms of space. So we talk about the future "lying ahead," or "behind," in some cultures. Or, we speak of a "landscape of possibilities," which is obviously a metaphor, but so common you almost don't notice it's a metaphor. And "possibility space" and "design space" are both frames that I find indispensable; we need some container for speaking about where all these intangible abstractions live – there has to be some way of describing, mapping, and articulating it. I'm very excited to see what happens if, or when, more landscape architects become interested in and attuned to the "landscape" of alternative futures.

AG I think so. Identifying where to intervene resonates. And that it doesn't all have to end up in one place, but could rather be distributed by nature, like putting pressure points on specific areas to allow that current to flow in a particular direction. This is also something that I ask of my students beyond the design: the consideration of which grounds to strategically plug into and the agents on the ground that might expand their ideas into other useful networks.

DARK
SPECULATION

PAUL DOBRASZCZYK

Paul Dobraszczyk is a lecturer in architecture at the Bartlett School of Architecture, University College London, and author of *Architecture and Anarchism* (2021), *Future Cities: Architecture and the Imagination* (2019), and *The Dead City: Urban Ruins and the Spectacle of Decay* (2017).

+ ARCHITECTURE, CINEMA, AESTHETICS

In January 2013, a photograph of a projected image on a smog-enshrouded high-rise building in Beijing became an internet sensation because it seemed uncannily reminiscent of the urban landscape seen in the 1982 film *Blade Runner*. Soon after, self-penned *Blade Runner* tours were being offered to tourists to cash in on this unexpected coming together of life and art, of the real and the imagined – a situation that has no doubt only intensified after the 2017 release of the film's much-lauded sequel *Blade Runner 2049*. We might be justifiably outraged by such an aestheticizing of urban pollution – toxic air that, after all, has a disastrous effect on those who must live with it day-by-day. What could be more disrespectful than a visiting tourist enjoying the very thing that makes residents suffer? Surely, it is dangerous to be lured into a seductive vision of the future that prioritizes aesthetic effect over embodied experience, surface over depth, the imagined over the real?

Here, I want to try to hold fire and sit with the discomfiting mingling of the imaginary and the real that we so often experience in cities today, where digital images coalesce with the physical built environment, whether on small or big screens. I'll focus on what are generally termed dystopian or post-apocalyptic imaginings of cities, principally because it is these ostensibly dark visions of the future that have come under fire from critics since at least the mid-1960s, when Susan Sontag published her powerful essay "The imagination of disaster." Sontag's argument was that dead cities in disaster cinema of the 1950s invited viewers to gain a "dispassionate, aesthetic view of destruction," thereby releasing them from any moral obligation to confront "what is psychologically unbearable," namely the *reality* of such mass destruction.[1]

More recently, cultural geographer Erik Swyngedouw has argued that apocalyptic imaginaries of climate change are tools that domesticate communal fears and prevent meaningful political action because they impose an idea of pure negativity on the world, the prospect of total extinction.[2] However, popular spectacles of apocalyptic destruction, particularly cinematic ones, have always been much more varied and complex than either Sontag and Swyngedouw have acknowledged, making it problematic to generalize about the effects they have on their audiences.[3] As the technical sophistication of computer-generated imagery (CGI) increases, so too does the range of opportunities for visualizing spectacles of urban destruction, particularly in cinema and video games. Increasingly realistic representations of dead cities such as New York in *I am Legend* (2007) and London in *The Girl with All the Gifts* (2016) can open up spaces of stillness that are valuable for new forms of thinking to emerge, precisely because these representations suspend in the imagination the mechanisms that sustain capitalism and its ideology of progress. Indeed, some critics have argued that only if capitalism and its urban centers of production are *already* imagined in ruins can such new thinking emerge, whether in a practice of salvage that remakes the world out of its ruins,[4] new forms of time that emancipate us from the constricting linear and "productive" time of capitalism,[5] or returns to past traumas in order to work through them toward healing.[6]

In this short essay, I want to explore three themes that can emerge from such imagined spaces of ruination: first, the relationship between aesthetics and the "real," which serves to question the basis of Sontag and others' critiques; second, the possibility of human thinking being open to more-than-human existence; and third, the suggestion of a more truthful form of production, namely one that incorporates entropy and decay rather than holding to the pervasive capitalist idea of progress and endless accumulation.

The Aesthetic Real

Both speculative realism, which came to the fore in the early 2000s, and its more recent offshoot object-oriented ontology have sought to challenge the basis of Western philosophy since Immanuel Kant – that is, that reality only exists in a meaningful way as and when it relates to human thought (known as "correlationism"). On the face of it, such anthropocentrism appears absurd – after all, it seems so obvious that things like animals and plants and rocks exist despite us. Yet, to acknowledge that things other than the human really do exist–or rather, that they exist equally to the human–creates a deep philosophical problem, for it directly challenges our supposed ability to gain exhaustive knowledge about the world outside of the human (a claim that is often made by science). For object-oriented ontologists, the solution is to accept that all things exist equally and that human knowledge of other things can only ever be partial rather than exhaustive. Graham Harman and Timothy Morton have gone further, arguing that this partial knowledge is much more akin to aesthetic experience than to empirical observation, and that it is aesthetic perception that actually precedes scientific method.[7] In their estimation, the way things in the world relate to each other is always at a distance, because equal existence implies that one thing can never know another exhaustively.

If we accept such a proposition–and even some scientists, particularly in the fields of quantum mechanics and cosmology, are beginning to do so–there are profound implications for the role of speculation in design. Let's return to the two images that introduced this essay: the smog-shrouded building in Beijing and the imaginary future Los Angeles of *Blade Runner*. Following Harman and Morton, we might now argue that the pleasure gained here from associating something real with something imagined is not somehow in opposition to an ethical consideration of the "real" effects of urban pollution, but rather *in excess* of it. Here, the two images generate a correspondence that expands the meanings of the urban beyond the conventional definitions of cause and effect (as we would expect when thinking about urban pollution). It's not that ethics is not a part of this correspondence or that it has somehow been sidelined, but rather that it becomes just one element in the expansion of meaning that happens when such correspondences occur.

Interestingly, it seems that Sontag modified her 1960s critique of the aestheticizing of disaster in the wake of the 9/11 terrorist attacks on New York. In 2003, she defended those who found sublime beauty in photographs of Ground Zero.[8] For Sontag, distancing the tragedy and finding beauty in images of the terrible ruins of 9/11 offered a vital corrective to both the desire to "fix" the meanings of the terrorist attacks and also, more generally, the sheer quantity of images of destruction we are now expected to process (and this before the internet came of age). Here, standing back and thinking about traumatic ruins–allowing imaginative correspondences to emerge–is not done in order to escape from or gain distance from everyday perception, but rather to return to it with an enlarged sympathy.

This kind of contemplative gaze might seem inimical to the creation of architecture, if we accept that design fundamentally rests in the transformation of an imaginative project into a material one (as, for example, architect Peter Zumthor does in his book *Thinking Architecture*). Surely, when the construction industry contributes so much to global warming and ecological devastation, taking the pedal off architectural production would be a beneficial move. Perhaps design might stay within the realm of the imaginary for much longer than it currently does, with designers developing the capacity for openness to the kinds of correspondences that emerge in this often-neglected milieu of human experience. Then, architects would be producers of possibilities rather than just material objects.

The World Without Us

One of the central aims of speculative realism and object-oriented ontology is to challenge anthropocentrism – the belief that humankind is the measure of all things. In this light, it is instructive to consider a longstanding thought experiment – the imagination of the world without humans. The disanthropic imagination originated in the early-19th century resurgence of millennial Christianity in the United States, coupled with the discovery and popularization of geological and evolutionary "deep time."[9] With the rise in ecological awareness since the 1970s, the contemporaneous threat of nuclear annihilation and the more recent prospect of mass extinction–not least our own-through catastrophic climate change, global pandemics, or overpopulation, the disanthropic imagination has flourished. In the 1970s, this was witnessed in Hal Lindsey and Carole C. Carlon's Christian millennialist bestseller *The Late Great Planet Earth* (1970) and in James Lovelock's influential Gaia hypothesis, in which the Earth carries on flourishing without humankind. In the first decade of this century it was seen in Alan Weisman's best-selling book *The World Without Us* (2007), and in televisual and cinematic renderings of the world without humans, such as *The Future is Wild* (2002), *Life after People* (2008), *Aftermath: Population Zero* (2008), and the Disney/Pixar animated film *Wall•E* (2008). More recently, the national lockdowns experienced by so many during the COVID-19 pandemic saw many cities seemingly emptied of human activity; and some saw this uncanny emptiness already foretold in fiction, for example, the deserted London in the 2002 film *28 Days Later* referenced by many during the first nationwide lockdown in the UK in April 2020.[10]

In disanthropic fantasies, a self-contradictory notion is at work: that is, a post-human Earth that can be imagined when, in fact, this imagining always requires a (human) spectator to be witness to its supposed absence.[11] According to Slovenian philosopher Slavoj Žižek (not a fan of speculative realism), disanthropic fantasies represent the reduction of the human subject to a "pure disembodied gaze observing our own absence" – a conceit that utterly fails to take account of our individual and collective responsibility for our long-term impact on the geosphere, whether we are around to witness it or not.[12] But that's precisely the point being made in *Wall•E*, where the eponymous robot is left alone to gather and compact the vast quantities of waste of humans who have rendered the city, and the world beyond, uninhabitable. As well as collecting certain discarded materials that appeal to the robot's anthropocentric nostalgia and desire to organize, *Wall•E* builds new skyscrapers out of the blocks of compacted waste, in effect creating a new skyline for the city as its former high-rises succumb to the processes of decay. Remarkable for a children's film, *Wall•E* uses an anthropomorphized robot as a lure – a metaphorical stand-in for humans who have abandoned their responsibility to the planet. Even more surprising is the fact that the film

challenges the hubris of capitalism's belief in containing its own unbridled wastes – the longed-for closed cycle of making and unmaking that remains a pervasive illusion of the ideology of capitalist growth.

Imagining the world without humans can also lead to a greater sensitivity to the increasingly destructive impact of human design on the planet. British naturalist Richard Jefferies was a pioneer in this respect in his 1884 fantasia *After London*. An elegiac meditation on loss, *After London* imagines an ecological disaster–the cause unspecified–that results in the inundation of London and half of England by sea and river waters, creating an enormous inland lake and a return to a pre-industrial life of subsistence farming, peasantry, and medieval chivalric codes of honor, not unlike the utopian vision of William Morris in *News from Nowhere* (1890), which Jeffries's novel inspired. *After London* is remarkable for the forensic way in which it describes the recolonization of London and the wider countryside by untamed nature, from the first plants springing up in cracked pavements to the overtaking of the entire city by dense vegetation and hordes of wild animals.[13] Indeed, so meticulous are the descriptions in the novel that, in 1996, the *New Scientist* asked leading botanists, animal ethnologists and material scientists to reconsider Jeffries's thought experiment, the result confirming its remarkable level of accuracy as well as its application to the modern urban built environment of concrete and steel.[14]

But there's a much darker element to Jefferies's imagination of the future. In contrast to the verdant countryside, the London of the book's title has become a deadly toxic wasteland: a "vast stagnant swamp," where the jet-black waters were topped with "a greenish-brown floating scum" – a toxic residue created by the city's crumbling buildings, millions of rotting corpses, and all the waste and sewage of the once great metropolis.[15] Jefferies's vision projects forward some of the intractable problems of the late-19th century city, most notably its reliance on a massive underground network of sewers built in the 1860s to remove the waste generated by its huge population. *After London* reveals how vulnerable the city's infrastructure might be if left unmaintained and also, in that state, how hidden networks like sewers might themselves contribute to a future catastrophe.

Visions of a world without humans offer a vital corrective to the hubris of designers, in particular their assumption that their products will contribute to a progressive improvement in urban life. Waste becoming buildings in *Wall•E* and sewers aiding the city's downfall in *After London* reverse conventional understandings of the future by calling attention to the unintended consequences of human-built projects. It is not just

that anthropocentrism blinds us to the impact of human activity on the more-than-human world, but that it also short circuits our ability to anticipate it biting back in the future. Nothing we build escapes influence from the more-than-human, however much it seems separated from it. In reality, the things that we make are always enmeshed in other things that we have little or no control over. The disanthropic imagination enables us to at least bring this sobering truth to mind.

Entropic Design

What if the world without humans was somehow already present in the here and now? A theme that runs throughout imaginative engagements with disaster and ruins is that of entropy, or the notion that matter, if left alone, will likely become more and more disordered and "ruined" over time, an exemplar material in this respect being sand. In relation to architecture, entropy indicates that buildings are always on the verge of ruin, with only the unceasing work of maintenance preventing it. Thus, entropy tends to posit ruins as both *future* oriented (always on the verge of happening) and as processes rather than objects (that is, ruin as a verb rather than a noun). The work of American artist Robert Smithson and his obsession with entropy has been influential for a generation of architects, artists, and critics interested in future-orientated conceptions of ruins. Smithson's 1967 article "The Monuments of Passaic" saw him travel through the post-industrial landscape of New

Jersey conjuring mythic time-scapes out of the remains of half-constructed motorways, industrial detritus, and car parks. Here, Smithson coined the term "ruins in reverse" to describe incomplete or abandoned structures.[16] Along with novelist J.G. Ballard and a host of subsequent artists, Smithson has forged fertile imaginative readings of "new" ruins, ones that have much to contribute to architecture and urban planning.

A politically charged example of such engagement is architect Jonathan Gales's short film *Megalomania*, released in 2014 by his animation studio Factory Fifteen. Here, the whole of London has become a vast construction site, with all of its buildings caught in a state of arrested development that could result in either future completion or irreversible decay.[17] In this seemingly abandoned city, the London Eye has grown informal appendages, while a giant skyscraper structure pictured at the end of the film is in fact an enormous assemblage of different construction elements: scaffolding, cranes, cladding panels, and a concrete frame. Inspired by the sudden collapse of the global construction industry in the wake of the 2007–2008 financial crisis, which temporarily halted the building of now iconic buildings like London's Shard and Dubai's Burj Khalifa, not to mention countless areas of new housing across Europe, *Megalomania* exaggerates the time-lag between a building's construction and completion in order to flag how vulnerable architecture is to fluctuations in the flows of global capital.[18]

In visualizing an entire city as a petrified construction site, the film asks if unfinished buildings might become the norm rather than the exception in our future cities and how we might go about salvaging their remains to produce something useful and inhabitable.

When what is conventionally regarded as architectural "failure" is completely recast, we are left questioning the very nature of architectural production itself. And this is no bad thing, given that it is the overarching ideology of building that is arguably at the root of its ecological destructiveness. In their 2014 book *Buildings Must Die*, Stephen Cairns and Jane M. Jacobs have taken architecture to task for its obsession with what they term "natalism"–the "birth" of a creative idea or building–at the expense of architectural ends, the (often well hidden) wasting and decay of buildings that accompany capitalist accumulation.

Breaking the bond between architecture and capitalism is not a utopian fantasy; rather, it is an urgent necessity given the dire warnings of climate scientists and ecologists. Appreciating the "wasting" of architecture–its incipient entropy, its ruins (old or new) that litter the planet, and its own productive excesses and attendant wastes–foregrounds another side of design, that of its inevitable ruin. Imagining these ends of architecture is precisely what can bring it back from the brink because it shatters the pervasive illusion of permanence that still exerts such a hold on designers – permanence of their ideas and of the things they create. Whether we're open to an expanded notion of the real, the imagination of disaster, or the inescapable force of entropy, imagining a future in ruins is not indicative of morbid fantasies taking hold, but rather the very opposite, holding out the hope of a painful liberation that comes from opening oneself up to the truth.

1 Susan Sontag, "The Imagination of Disaster" (1965) in *Against Interpretation* (London, 1994), 216, 225.

2 Erik Swyngedouw, "Apocalypse Forever? Post-political Popularism and the Spectre of Climate Change," *Theory Culture Society* 27 (2010): 213–30; and "Apocalypse Now! Fear and Doomsday Pleasure," *Capitalism Nature Socialism* 24, no. 1 (2013): 9–18.

3 See Mick Broderick, "Surviving Armageddon: Beyond the imagination of disaster," *Science Fiction Studies* 20, no. 3 (1993): 362–82.

4 See Evan Calder Williams, *Combined and Uneven Apocalypse* (Winchester, 2011) for an elucidation of the meanings of what he terms "salvagepunk."

5 Bruce Braun & Stephanie Wakefield, "Inhabiting the Post-apocalyptic City," *Society and Space* 32, no. 1 (2014).

6 See, for example, Anirban Kapil Baishya, "Trauma, Post-apocalyptic Science Fiction and the Post-human," *Wide Screen* 3, no. 1 (2011): 1–25.

7 See, for example, Graham Harman, *Object-Oriented Ontology: A New Theory of Everything* (Penguin, 2018); and Timothy Morton, *Being Ecological* (Penguin, 2018).

8 Susan Sontag, *Regarding the Pain of Others* (London, 2003), 67–68.

9 Greg Garrard, "Worlds Without Us: Some types of disanthropy," *SubStance* 127 (2012): 40–42.

10 See Paul Dobraszczyk, "Empty Cities Have Long Been a Post-apocalyptic Trope – Now, they are a Reality," *The Conversation* (January 18, 2021), https://theconversation.com/empty-cities-have-long-been-a-post-apocalyptic-trope-now-they-are-a-reality-153263.

11 Garrard, "Worlds Without Us," 43.

12 Slavoj Žižek, *Living in the End Times* (Verso, 2010), 80.

13 Jefferies's description of nature overtaking London and the rest of England occupies the first section of *After London; or, Wild England* (Duckworth & Co., 1905; original, 1884), 1–12.

14 See Laura Spinney, "Return to Paradise," *New Scientist* (July 20, 1996), 26–31.

15 Jefferies, *After London*, 32.

16 The article, which also included Smithson's photographs, was originally published as "The Monuments of Passaic," *Artforum* (December 1967), 52–57.

17 The film can be viewed at https://vimeo.com/38091515.

18 On architectural incompletion as ruins, see Paul Dobraszczyk, *The Dead City: Urban Ruins and the Spectacle of Decay* (Bloomsbury Publishing, 2017), 189–213.

CHRISTOPHER MARCINKOSKI
SUBJECT v. METHOD

From the beginning of the antibiotic age, humans knew it would be a temporary arrangement. Endlessly versatile transformers and producers, microbes would continuously evade human control. Microbes have no morals; they are neither enemies nor friends. Learning to live with them brought new ways of life, but also a re-cultivation of wonder, a recognition of our place in the cosmos.[1]

Christopher Marcinkoski is an associate professor of landscape architecture and urban design at the University of Pennsylvania and founding partner of PORT – a public realm and urban design practice. He is author of *The City That Never Was* (2016) and a fellow of the American Academy in Rome.

+ DESIGN, EDUCATION

In December 2019, Zuzanna Drozdz, a master's student in landscape architecture at the University of Pennsylvania, presented her final project prepared as part of the "A Greater Bay Area?" studio.[2] Titled "Synth-Ethic-Bio-City," Drozdz's project imagined an urban future for Guangzhou, China, circa 2049 following on a hypothetical pandemic that struck China in 2029. The project, developed over the course of the Fall 2019 semester, elaborated an urban form and corresponding lifestyle that emerged from a reimagining of modern medicine and public health protocols that abandoned pursuit of the total control of microbes—the so-called "war on germs"—and embraced the active cultivation of the city's microbiome across scales, from the individual to the metropolitan, as a fundamental consideration of future urban governance.

> Officials began to culture myriad complex communities of bacteria, archaea, fungi, and viruses—with a focus on their various interrelationships—throughout the city. The Ministry of Health incentivized residents to actively maintain their individual microbiomes to improve the collective health of the city. The personal pursuit of a properly balanced microbiome became understood as a matter of service to the nation. In turn, Guangzhou's new-found respect for microbial power engendered a creative revolution that transformed long-held notions of urban metabolism as they related to daily life.[3]

As we all now know, a pandemic that changes the way we occupy our cities isn't a hypothetical, it didn't wait until 2029, and it wasn't limited to China. Thus, it is not hyperbole to say that a mere three months after this final studio presentation, the world would be fundamentally changed – forever.[4] Yet I don't highlight Drozdz's project for its prescience—though the coincidence is uncanny—but rather to emphasize what I see as the potential value in a design pedagogy that engages with the future as a set of plausible possibilities rather than concerning oneself solely with the conspicuous challenges of today.

At a moment where seemingly any design work that is not actively attempting to resolve one or more of the myriad crises

Opposite: Yang Du (2019).

facing humanity and the planet is dismissed as unserious or even an unethical waste of resources–particularly within landscape architectural education–I would like to use this essay to mount an argument against the veneration of solutionism increasingly evident within design pedagogy. Central to this proposition is positioning the consideration of speculation–in multiple forms–as being of central concern to 21st-century landscape architectural education and practice.

Though many of the central actors engaged with Speculative Design (aka Critical Design, aka Design Fiction) that came out of or orbited around Fiona Raby and Anthony Dunne's work at the Royal College of Art in London in the years following the 2008–2009 global financial crisis have more or less sworn the agenda off as being too easily bound up with capitalism and the neo-liberal project, I would argue that for those disciplines concerned with the making of the built environment this fundamental correlation between capital, city making, and speculative practices is not a dire deficiency, but rather an untapped opportunity. Allow me to explain.

I came to an intellectual and scholarly engagement with speculation not through an uncommon interest in designerly creativity, but rather via a critical consideration of planning and design's complicity in the global real estate boom and bust that led to the financial crisis mentioned above. Here my own concerns with the subject of speculation related to the built environment–global real estate practices and speculative urbanization specifically–and the catastrophic social, environmental, and politico-economic consequences of what I saw as a rapidly proliferating phenomenon.[5] My interest was in the role design and planning played–both intentionally and unintentionally–in advancing these often-ruinous activities. This work focused on retooling urban design practice toward a fundamental concern with the near-term initiation of these activities, in contrast to the long-standing preoccupation with preferred outcome.

At the same time, much of the recent scholarship on speculation from disciplines outside of the built environment also came on the heels of the global financial crisis. Publications like Vyjayanthi Rao, Carin Kuoni, and Prem Krishnamurthy's *Speculation, Now: Essays and Artwork* (Duke University Press, 2015), Dunne and Raby's *Speculative Everything* (MIT Press, 2013), and Alex Wilkie, Martin Savransky, and Marsha Rosengarten's *Speculative Research: The Lure of Possible Futures* (Routledge, 2017) all took up and recast notions of speculation as means of critical practice undertaken in direct opposition to the politico-economic policies, transactions, and machinations that precipitated the events which catalyzed this work. Here, the possibility of conceptualizing worlds, actions, and theories from beyond the familiar politics and economics

Anni Lei (2018).

Zuzanna Drozdz (2019).

became the focus of intellectual and scholarly production from disciplines as varied as anthropology, journalism, ethnographic studies, theology, finance, fashion, literature, and geography, to name but a few.

Yet at the same time, few within the built-environment disciplines mounted comparable reflections – self-preservation necessitates that one not bite the hand that feeds it. Rather, in the years that immediately followed the financial crisis, the capital driving speculative urbanization simply found new destinations for investment—principally in emerging economies—before eventually returning to more mature economies as the global economy recovered a few years later. The built-environment disciplines largely bided their time during this recessionary period, seemingly hoping for a return to the halcyon days of speculative building pre-2008. Their patience was, as we know, rewarded.

Recognizing the cyclical nature of real-estate speculation, the focus of my initial research and studio teaching was on engaging its forces through the elaboration of strategies for the planning and design of new forms of development that could (potentially) inflect or influence the economic and political drivers behind these projects on their own terms, from within the existing system. Specifically considering aspects of value and risk, this work focused principally on approaches to the initiation of new settlement – that is, how to reach a critical mass of viability as quickly as possible from both the urbanistic and economic perspective, while simultaneously prioritizing the environmental and social performance of these new settlement products. Such approaches were both nimble and contingent, privileging the early stages of urbanization activities. However, while the priority here was on the processes of physical urbanization, the orienting drivers and resultant forms of the strategies of urbanization elaborated within design studios often remained familiar.

Upon reflection, I concluded that what was being produced within my studios was symptomatic of something that I was observing—and continue to observe—more broadly within landscape architectural education. That is, a preoccupation with problem solving and world saving in lieu of engaging with the design of landscapes as a creative and experimental practice capable of posing questions, provoking dialogue, and encouraging reflection on other possibilities. The work was stunted by a privileging of landscape architecture's perceived subservience to science and engineering over its more open-ended connections to culture, creative practice, and the humanities. The reasons for such a preoccupation within the discipline—particularly in the American context—are legion, and there is not space here to identify and unpack each of them. In synopsis however, my sense is that this desire to "world

Shuhan Liu (2018).

save" drives a disciplinary reliance on known strategies, the rehearsing of familiar forms and aesthetics, and the limiting of engagement to a narrow band of project types.

As a means of responding to this reality in my own teaching, I began contemplating studio prompts that were simply unanswerable. Premises that demanded the invention of methods to engage since familiar approaches lacked any meaningful resonance. This led to the development of studios rooted in circumstances and geographies so broad and so complicated that the only way to take them up was through the consideration of a single particular thread within the weft and warp of their emerging reality. For me, that thread is the public realm of future urban form.

The student project described above was a product of this work. Beginning in 2018, I led two studios that considered China's then recently introduced Greater Bay Area (GBA) initiative as a point of departure for undertaking intensive, semester-long, design-investigations that considered the socio-cultural potentials of the future urban forms that might result from this initiative. With the stated aspirations of the GBA project vis-à-vis technological innovation—artificial intelligence, data collection, automation, surveillance, advanced manufacturing—in mind, the studio's primary preoccupation was the consideration of potential influences and implications of this technologically-enabled

destiny on the physical form and socio-spatial characteristics of the Pearl River Delta. Specifically, the form and identity of the public realms of the GBA's extant urban centers, circa 2049 – the centenary of the founding of the People's Republic of China.

Unsurprisingly, in all the bureaucratic policy language of the GBA plan, very little attention is paid to questions of cultural or physical identity of urban form within the proposed mega-region. So, while Rem Koolhaas's late 1990s study of the Pearl River Delta, *Project on the City I: Great Leap Forward*,[6] was organized around six almost impossibly broad themes–ideology, architecture, money, landscape, policy, and infrastructure–our studio considered and engaged one single, essential aspect of urban space and form where these broad considerations intersect: the urban public realm of the future GBA.

As a means of achieving a productive rupture with present-day conventions of design thinking and representation, these studios chose to operate utilizing tools of expression beyond the disciplinarily familiar plan, section, elevation, and axonometric. Instead, written narrative, short animated film, and physical artifact became the medium for studio work in speculative world-building. In lieu of a preoccupation with comprehensive–engineering-like–descriptions of near-term solutions, the designerly capacity for describing and elaborating space was employed in the production of episodic depictions of future urban possibilities. This methodology unapologetically riffs on Dunne and Raby's "United Micro Kingdoms" project. It aims to bring the methods and practice of speculative world-building into landscape architecture pedagogy as means to imagine social, environmental, and geo-political possibilities beyond the known or the familiar.

In addition to a post-pandemic, pro-microbial Guangzhou (Drozdz), these studios produced urban fictions as varied as a society in which every person at birth is assigned a cuddly cat-like companion drone as means of concealing omnipresent surveillance behind a veil of cuteness (Farre Nixon); a hybrid technology/real estate product that allows for artificial reality engagement with deceased family members in perpetuity as a means of allowing a country's population to "live forever" (Anni Lei); and a post-labor society where creativity and imagination become the principal currency and means of defining social hierarchy and political status (Lindsay Burnette).

These assorted design fictions—which take up issues of labor, health, privacy, creativity, nostalgia, and social-cohesion, among other concerns—intentionally do not offer answers to specified problems. Instead, they bring to the fore subjects of consideration not often engaged within built environment design pedagogy and use the physical design of urban form and space as a means of telling particular, often idiosyncratic,

stories. The pedagogical intent is to generate new or novel points of view as a means of considering the existential challenges facing humanity from perspectives other than the known or the familiar. The work looks to use multiple stories of possible futures as a means of holding a mirror up to the realities and presumptions of the present day.

The design fictions from the first incarnation of this studio were selected for inclusion in the central pavilion of the 2019/2020 *Bi-City Biennale of Urbanism\Architecture* in Shenzhen, curated by Italian architect and urbanist Carlo Ratti. The theme of the Biennale—which considered how digital technologies are impacting urban life—offered an ideal platform to share this studio work. However, just before the exhibition was set to open, the work was removed due to its particular subject matter. While disappointing, this also suggested to me the importance of what had been accomplished. That is, the exclusion confirmed that these design fictions offer critical means of engaging with important subjects of socio-urban and environmental concern. So important that they might even be deemed too provocative for general public consumption.

Of course, the 2019/2020 Bi-City *Biennale of Urbanism\ Architecture* was ultimately disrupted by the COVID-19 pandemic. And like everyone else, I was forced into a period of pandemic-induced self-reflection. As I considered the arc of

Farre Nixon (2018).

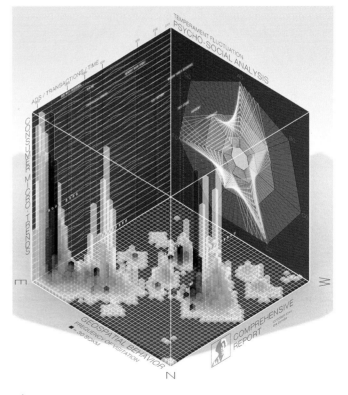

my option studio teaching and design research over the prior four years–moving from speculative urbanization as a subject to pedagogical experiments with critical design speculation as method–I began to consider whether there was a way to bring the two research areas into dialogue. So, with the extreme isolation induced by the global pandemic as intellectual cover, 14 graduate students studying across four time zones in three countries in the fall semester of 2020 joined me in the pursuit.

Specifically, this incarnation of the studio in Fall 2020 used the proliferation of speculative urbanization practices across the African continent seen over the last 15 years as the subject of consideration. This is a topic with which I have been engaged in various forms but has principally related to the documentation and exhibition of more than 100 examples of proposals for large-scale green-field development at the periphery of existing urban centers.[7] These projects–promoted by both public and private actors–share many of the same characteristics seen in the speculative urbanization activities that led to the global financial crisis of the first decade of this century; the principal difference being the scale and frequency of what is being proposed and, in turn, the potentially catastrophic environmental and socio-economic impacts of these ongoing activities.

Unlike the GBA studios, this version of the studio utilized a shared origin story from which individual projects were asked to depart. There is not space here to describe the entirety of this fiction, but the principal plot points are a continent, circa 2050, that is fully decoupled from the known world order. A truly Pan-African form of governance has been established and has chosen this intentional decoupling as a conscious response to climate-change induced global catastrophes. The full self-sufficiency and sovereignty of the African continent has been achieved by home-grown advances in communications technology and artificial intelligence that allow for the pursuit of a truly collective enterprise of 2.5-billion people. And as part of this technological innovation, novel formats of settlement and infrastructure–not to mention cultivation and conservation practices–have been developed across the continent in direct response to local physiographic and cultural considerations. The result is a multiplicity of future urban forms.

The pedagogical purpose of this fictional premise is a belief in the necessity of a conceptual rupture with the present geo-political reality in order to fully liberate student thinking on the formats and orientations that might characterize future urban form. Without this break, the work of the studio risked becoming an extension of the world as we know it today, leaving the so-called futures being elaborated as inevitably familiar. Certainly, there are great risks in asking a group of graduate students who are principally Western or Asian in upbringing and education to contemplate future urban form and public life on the African continent. However, in framing this thought experiment through the alternative value system described in the origin story above, the intention was to have students confront and problematize their own preconceptions about what future urban form might entail. Central to this reflection is a rejection of the treatment of the African continent–and by extension, the so-called "African City"– as a monolithic whole.[8]

Depending on the source, as many as 25 of the 100 largest metropolitan areas in the world, circa 2050, will be located on the African continent. By cross-referencing population projections with the eight principal biomes present on the continent, the studio identified 15 metropolitan areas available for consideration by students. While spread across countries characterized by a range of politico-economic conditions, the studio was expressly interested in the array of bio-climatic, cultural, and physiographic contexts in which these future megalopolises would be constructed. It is the collision of these diverse ecological and cultural conditions with the impending production of new urban settlement at the edges of existing metropolitan areas that is the central focus of the work.

The studio intentionally embraced our remoteness that semester by considering multiple, divergent contexts, and set them into dialogue with one another rather than collectively contemplating a single site. Thus, each of the 14 students who participated was invited to come to know a specific geography with which they likely had little, if any, prior relationship or ability to visit. The studio utilized the consideration of future hypothetical public realms as a device for reflecting on the potential nature of an urbanity and society that is fundamentally different from what is known today. The source of this difference could be technological, environmental, or economic. Regardless, the nature of these imagined urban landscapes was understood as a manifestation of a future society's possible values. Like the GBA studios that came before it, the studio endeavored to produce visual and textual narratives that asked questions and challenged established norms about future urban settlement, rather than provide specific answers to existing problems.

This studio work took up the extremes of water – its absence in Johannesburg and its relentless encroachment in Lagos (Fangyuan Sheng, Mingyang Sun, and Gi-chul Choe). Cairo was imagined to finally be fully abandoned in favor of occupying yet another New Cairo (Yi Ding and Di Hu). Future settlement practices in Nairobi and Khartoum were imagined as transient and cyclical – driven by seasonal-based infrastructures in the former, and the cross-cultural ritual celebration of food in the latter (Zien Chen, Qinyuan Tan, Aaron Stone, and Keke Huang). Elsewhere, the future peri-urban form of Addis Ababa was imagined through the lens of biodiversity, and an ever-growing Kinshasa was considered through the lens of La Sape–the *Société des Ambianceurs et des Personnes Élégantes*–and its long-standing connection to the anti-colonial movements of the early 20th century (Tone Chu, Bingjian Lui, and Yufei Yan).

The virtual nature of this studio elevated the importance of the short, animated films as the principal product of the design research. In this regard, the study of extant visual culture and the invention of new aesthetics became a preoccupation of

Mingyang Sun + Fangyuan Sheng (2020).

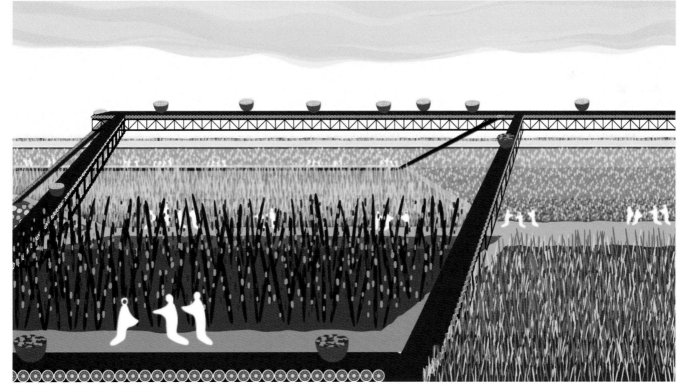

Aaron Stone + Keke Huang (2020).

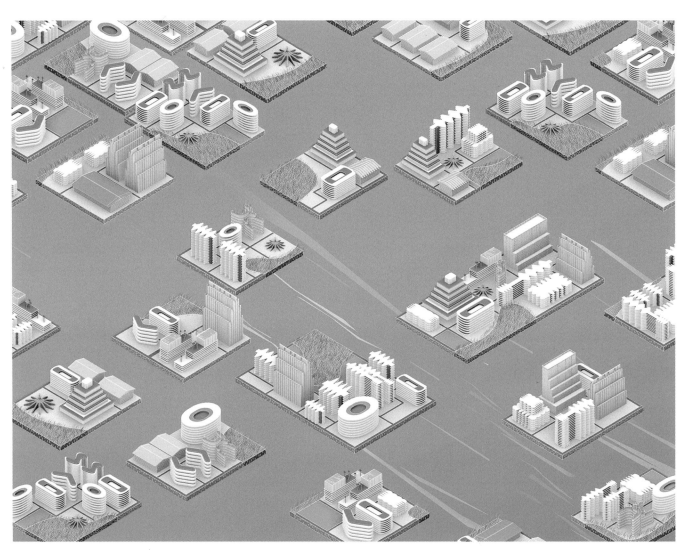

Bingjian Lui + Yufei Yan (2020).

the studio. Grasping the texture and character of a place after a short visit–as was the case with the earlier GBA studios–is daunting and fraught with hazard. Attempting to come to a comparable understanding of a place that one has never visited is a near impossible task. For this studio, that impossibility was precisely the pedagogical utility of the endeavor.

Of course, after four years of these kinds of studios one is compelled to ask: what is the value of considering and engaging with various forms of speculation as they relate to the making of the built environment? What disciplinary role does speculation play or should it play? Does the consideration of speculation have application beyond the pedagogical incubator of the studio? Is it possible to understand critical design speculation as a creative, productive activity capable of standing in opposition to dominant neoliberal urbanization practices? Or is the making of the built environment simply so bound up with capital that speculation, in any form, serves as nothing more than a destructive and extractive operation? The answer, of course, is that it is all these things, and likely many more.

From my perspective, there is power in this multiplicity. It demands recognition that there are manifold futures available, and that design's responsibility is enabling this multiplicity, rather than operating in pursuit of a single, preferred outcome. Speculation seen this way portends possibilities and rejects answers. It provides both design pedagogy and design practice with a potentially powerful form of engagement, offering a means of initiating conversation and encouraging reflection. Here, speculation represents a medium for designers and–more importantly–non-designers to imagine and occupy other possible circumstances through storytelling and narrative, both written and visual. This embrace of speculation allows us to understand design not just a means to solve or optimize or extract, but as a framework for contemplation, for thinking through what is possible – the good and the bad, the utopian and the dystopian. And every future in between.

1 Zuzanna Drozdz, "Synth-Ethic-Bio-City," studio project, University of Pennsylvania (2019).

2 This was one of three studios focusing on Asia at the Weitzman School of Design generously supported by funding from AECOM.

3 Ibid.

4 We now know that COVID-19 began to emerge much earlier than this, but it only began to receive regular media attention in the US in January 2020.

5 This includes my 2016 book, *The City That Never Was* (Princeton Architectural Press, 2016), as well as essays in T*opos, Domus, LA+ Journal*, and *New Geographies*, among others.

6 Rem Koolhaas et al. (eds), *Project on the City I: Great Leap Forward* (Taschen, 2001).

7 This work has been exhibited in Malaysia (Kuala Lumpur Architecture Festival, 2017), Germany (Architekturgalerie Munich, 2018) and Italy (Politecnico di Milano, 2019).

8 Like the studios that came before it, the work that was produced as part of this incarnation of the studio has been awarded and included in various competitions and publications. This recognition can certainly be attributed to the creativity and spirit of the students who willingly undertook this adventure during the depths of the pandemic.

Alexandra Sankova

EVERYDAY

Alexandra Sankova is founding director of the Moscow Design Museum, which was established in 2012 with the mission to collect, preserve, and promote the design heritage of Russia. Exhibitions she has curated at the museum include *History of Russian Design 1917–2017*, and *Discovering Utopia: Lost Archives of Soviet Design,* which received the Utopia Medal at the London Design Biennale 2016. She is author of several books, including *23* (2010), *Cosmic Visions from the USSR* (2020), and *Designed in the USSR: 1950–1989* (2018).

✛ INDUSTRIAL DESIGN

Visual depictions of alien worlds and the means by which to reach them have not been limited to pulp magazines and cinema. For nearly a century governments have utilized extraterrestrial landscapes as a medium of political propaganda and promotion of science and technology. These speculative landscapes, and the imagined technologies enabling access to them, draw from aspects of architecture and urban design as much as from physics and engineering. Their capacity to captivate and cultivate a public imagination remains as resonant today as it did in the mid-20th century.

This essay considers the way the Soviet state instrumentalized acts of speculation related to space travel in order to infuse the Soviet people with a sense of pride and enthusiasm about their country's scientific and economic excellence relative to other countries. Elegantly disguised in the form of everyday items, this space-oriented propaganda advanced the idea of a bright communist future for everyone and the essential importance of collective labor. Cosmonauts were proclaimed national heroes and space exploration was situated at the top of the national agenda. Perceived superiority in outer space

charged the masses with enthusiasm, helping people come to terms with expectations of a rather modest life, hard work, and constant shortages, drawing the public's attention away from the imperfections of the existing political system.

In 1903 the Russian space visionary, philosopher, and inventor Konstantin Tsiolkovsky[1] published the first part of his research, "Jet Exploration of Global Outer Space," in the journal *Scientific Review* in which he offered detailed analysis and proof that flights into outer space were possible. Most readers dismissed these ideas as no more than the eccentric fantasies of a 46-year-old teacher from provincial Kaluga. However, Tsiolkovsky was undeterred and with fanatical stubbornness he continued his research into the design of rocket flight. Ultimately, Tsiolkovsky's work proved that unmanned balloons were extremely difficult to lift to an altitude of more than 22 km, and only multistage rockets would be able to break through the Earth's atmosphere. With this conclusion, Tsiolkovsky believed that it was only a matter of time before the Earth would be surrounded by human-made space stations contributing to various scientific and national economic purposes.[2]

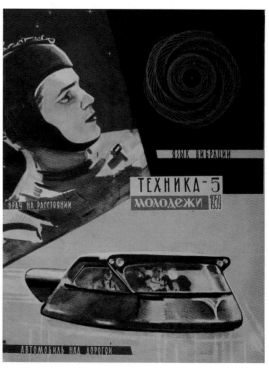

Tsiolkovsky published several pamphlets at his own expense– "Dreams of the Earth and the Sky," "On the Moon," "Jet Exploration of Outer Space"–hoping to draw the attention of opinion makers and public institutions to the importance of space exploration and the necessity of building piloted rockets. However, his publications went largely unnoticed, and it was only after the October Revolution of 1917 that Tsiolkovsky's research was finally widely recognized.

Following the October Revolution, the newly born Soviet state denied all values and achievements associated with Tsarist Russia. Everything from the way people thought to the way people lived had to change. In renouncing the old world, the Soviet state had also to invent and build a new one. This new socialist society called for new buildings, modern interiors, and the design and production of fabrics, clothing, household items, and furniture that would reflect the changed ideology of the Soviet person. Life was no longer private, but communal. The state took control of how ideas about the future would be developed. The bright future of the communist world was to be center stage in education, science, and culture.

"An illiterate person stands outside politics, he must first be taught the alphabet,"[3] Vladimir Lenin famously noted. Accordingly, during the first few years following the October Revolution the state made special efforts to raise national literacy levels by setting up free evening schools, reading rooms, libraries, and art and cultural centers. It was vital for the state to showcase the advancements and superiority of Soviet science, technology, and culture within the country. Printed publications became the most effective instruments of agitation and propaganda. According to statistics published in *Printing in the RSFSR* in 1922, popular science books significantly surpassed political literature in total circulation, with the total share of science-related publications at more than 35%.[4] While many publications focused on exploring the natural assets of Earth, many also considered the impending settlement of other planets, enticing the public with captivating ideas about the bright future of the communist world. In 1933, the legendary *Tekhnika Molodezhi* (Technology for the Youth) journal was founded, and to this day remains one of the leading popular science publications in Russia. Beginning as a purely technical publication, *Tekhnika Molodezhi* soon diversified its content to include works of Soviet and foreign science fiction.

The sci-fi illustrations of the 1920s and 1930s included in *Tekhnika Molodezhi* and other publications depicted endless possibilities of a great socialist future, advancement of technology, and innovations in all areas of science. In these stories, the Soviet people would build huge factories for the extraction and processing of minerals on asteroids. Celestial bodies would be controlled by thousands of nozzles from a distance of millions of kilometers, transporting mined materials from Mars or Venus. Artists dreamt of high-tech, multi-level cities whose inhabitants travelled in lightweight aircrafts. Personal mobility devices like "air bicycles" and "air motorcycles" would be a reality in no more than a decade.

Magazine illustrations fueled the imagination of Soviet citizens, motivating them to study and work harder to assure control of the natural assets of the Earth and other planets in the near future. In these stories the Soviet people would be the ones to design and create gyrocopters, monorails, flight control centers, and transport hubs in outer space. They would be the ones to instigate revolutions in alien civilizations, assuming they too struggled with class inequality. In reality, however, technologies developed at a much slower pace than the fantasies of artists and scientists, depending directly on the accumulation of Soviet military-industrial power.

These captivating visual and textual speculations shifted the attention of the everyday Soviet person away from their poor living conditions, high workloads, state inefficiency, and censorship by immersing readers in stories of fantastic extraterrestrial worlds and how other civilizations would be saved through communism. Alexei Tolstoy's novel "Aelita," published in *Krasnaya Nov* magazine in 1922–1923, is considered the first "space" book of early Soviet science fiction. In this story, enthusiastic genius Los (Elk) builds a rocket and, taking the Red Army soldier Gusev as a companion, sets off to Mars where they discover a civilization in decay. Los wins the heart of the beautiful princess Aelita, and Gusev, as befits a true communist, instigates a revolution. The book was turned into a silent feature film that premiered in 1924 and featured futuristic architecture and costumes of Martians that sharply contrasted with the drab daily realities of the Soviet people.

Protagonists of numerous other novels also traveled to outer space, where they too persuaded new civilizations to build communist societies and devise interplanetary revolutions. In Viktor Goncharov's dilogy *Interplanetary Traveler* and *Psychomachine* (1924), Leninist Young Communist League member Andrei and scientist Nikodim help locals start a revolution on the moon. In Nikolai Mukhanov's *The Burning Abyss* (1924), an interplanetary war is described for the first time, where Soviet people battle the ubiquitous Martians armed with laser weapons. Grail Arelsky's *The Tale of Mars* (1925) and Valery

Yazvitsky's *Journey to the Moon and Mars* (1928), among many others, describe encounters with an alien mind. Alexander Belyaev's novel *Leap into Nothing* (1933), which tells the story of an old-regime bourgeois who sets off on a spaceship known as "The Ark" to wait out a revolution on Earth, was praised by no less than Tsiolkovsky himself.

In 1928, Georgy Krutikov, a VKhUTEIN[5] architecture student, presented to the examination board his provocative project for a flying city. Inspired by Tsiolkovsky's designs, Krutikov proposed leaving the land for work and rest, moving everyday life to the airspace of uniform communal cities. In this project, Krutikov put forward a concept where each social formation generated its own typology of city: feudalism would produce a central radial layout with a fortress in the middle, while capitalism would have a perpendicular intersection of streets in a rectangular city plan. Communication between cities was to be carried out using individual flying cabins capable of movement in any environment: land, water, air, and atmosphere-less space. The droplet-shaped capsules were a universal unit of living space equipped with transformable furniture necessary for daily life. The mobile capsule could easily move through space using electromagnetic waves and connect to any of the floating buildings. Krutikov's project was widely and intensely discussed in the architectural community. Some considered the proposal to be the last word of science, turning a new page in the history of architecture. Others severely criticized him for excessive, otherworldly speculation.

Once Soviet cosmonaut Yuri Gagarin successfully completed the first manned flight into space in April 1961, images of a man in space quickly found their way to mainstream painting, sculpture, and print, showcasing cosmonauts controlling spaceships, looking through windows toward distant galaxies, and walking through the landscapes of other planets. These space-related technological breakthroughs continued to influence design, art, and literature. Coinciding with the "Khrushchev Thaw" of the 1960s when the "Iron Curtain" separating the USSR from the world was lifted, an intensifying optimism increasingly influenced artistic spheres within the Soviet state. Artworks on space themes were full of enthusiasm with visuals in bright, iridescent colors. Space was pictured as peaceful, and the inhabitants of other planets as generally positive creatures.

Space flight opened exciting, new perspectives for the Soviet people. New research and education institutes were created, with technological progress and scientific discoveries inspiring professionals across all fields. Art experienced a new wave of avant-garde with the orientation of artistic

production fundamentally changing. If in the 1950s artists were dreaming about the possibility that technological means would afford an extractive engagement with the vastness of the universe, then, less than a decade later, they were visualizing permanently inhabited star cities, cosmic greenhouses, and space stations characterized by a more collaborative coexistence. In 1962, space design became an official part of the state design system in Moscow with the *All-Union Scientific Research Institute of Technical Aesthetics* (VNIITE)[6] set up to oversee and lead industrial design in the USSR. VNIITE designers developed projects for the space industry, working closely with specialized domestic enterprises across the country.

As dreams of flying into space occupied the minds of the Soviet people, the interiors and exteriors of public buildings were increasingly filled with images of the distant universe and cosmonauts launching into space. The so-called "space style" took shape in Soviet architecture. Buildings resembled interplanetary ships and satellites. The shapes of planets, rockets, and improvised scientific stations appeared on playgrounds. The walls of kindergartens and schools were covered in stars and galaxies. New metro stations featured images of cosmonauts. Space themes dominated events across the country, offering entertainment to Soviet people and highlighting the latest achievements in science or the launch of a new spacecraft. Colorful posters with slogans such as "communists pave the way to the stars" and "science and communism are inseparable" were everywhere.

Achievements in space exploration became part of the grandiose propaganda system of the Soviet state. Soviet industrial designers created vacuum cleaners in the shape of rockets and satellites, textiles with space ornaments, themed Christmas tree decorations, toy rockets, and astronaut dolls. Space station names became brands of watches, cigarettes, and confectionary. For example, following a successful flight of the first Soviet cosmonaut on the "Vostok" spacecraft, mass production of a "Vostok" table clock was launched. The first batch was produced at Chelyabinsk Watch Factory "Molniya" (lightning) in 1961. Coincidentally, this same factory had previously produced devices for military and early space program needs. In the early 1970s, Konstantin Sobakin designed an electric samovar "Sputnik" that was mass produced at Suksun Metal Production Factory in Perm as part of their product diversification program. The "Sputnik" retained the functionality, but not the visuals of a traditional samovar. It was spherical, had a plastic "orbit" in place of handles, and its legs were narrowed cones reminiscent of the antennas of the first satellite launched in 1957. This samovar was often given as a gift to Western partners and Soviet cosmonauts.

Alongside design and architecture developments, there was a space speculation-driven upsurge in literature, cinema, and music. In 1956, Ivan Efremov's science fiction novel *The Andromeda Nebula* was published. It was the first book in the "cosmic series" describing a future Earth that joins a galactic community of civilizations called the "Great Ring." During 1950–70s brothers Arkady and Boris Strugatsky wrote many novels and short stories set beyond the orbit of Earth including *The Land of Crimson Clouds* (1959), *The Way to Amalthea* (1960), *Hard to Be God* (1963), *Inhabited Island* (1969), and many others. The Strugatsky brothers' main protagonists–astronauts–went through various trials, facing moral and ethical challenges while exploring extraterrestrial civilizations. Inspired by these books and stories, Soviet filmmakers created incredible science-fiction features and animations, with scientists and astronauts participating in an official capacity as consultants. Many of these films became true hits, often making it impossible to get tickets to the cinema screenings and leading generations of families, friends, and neighbors to gather around television sets when premieres were released.

In 1961, Alexander Kazantsev's novel *The Planet of Storms* was turned into a feature film.[7] It told a story of a joint Soviet-American expedition to Venus, where travelers met aliens who could read minds and transform into any creature. In *Moscow-Cassiopeia* (1973) scientists detected a radio signal of intelligent beings from a planet in the Shedar star system.[8] The Zarya spacecraft was built by a young inventor to reach the planet. However, since such a flight would last for several decades, prospective astronauts were recruited from among enthusiastic Soviet schoolchildren. This period also had great influence on scientific and technical publications. Many talented artists worked in publishing houses at the time and popular science journals became a haven for their creativity and an asylum for nonconformist[9] art. Journal editors were quite liberal in their attitudes toward this creative self-expression. As censorship focused first and foremost on text, visual depictions were often left untouched.

Beginning in the 1970s and extending into the 1980s, space fiction began to fade into the background of popular interest, yielding to the chronicles of the real space exploration program. Artworks created by cosmonauts and their coauthors and published mainly by *Molodaya Gvardiya* started to enjoy fame. *The Way to Mars* (1979), *On an Asteroid* (1984), and *Hello, Phobos!* (1988) by Evgeny Khrunov and Levon Khachaturyants,

and *Black Silence* (1987) by Yuri Glazkov were among the most popular. To depict spaceships and landscapes on other planets, artists increasingly studied scientific literature and consulted directly with experts. Thanks to this collaboration, illustrations were rife with believable detail, and distant worlds became even more realistic in representation.

Throughout the Soviet period of the 20th century, space exploration became a national idea that was broadcast everywhere. Superiority in outer space charged the masses with enthusiasm, distracted citizens from their rather modest lives, hard work, and constant shortages, serving to justify the imperfections of the political system. In total, from 1961 to 1991, 72 cosmonauts visited space with 68 men and two women awarded the honorary title of "Pilot-Cosmonaut of the USSR." Schools, streets, neighborhoods, and entire settlements were named after these space explorers, while portraits and sculptures of astronauts filled public spaces and museum exhibitions. Cosmonauts became role models for younger generations. They gave public talks to students and workers and interviews with cosmonauts were regularly published in leading Soviet newspapers and magazines.

In a 1962 issue of *Technika Molodezhi*, an open letter was published on behalf of Soviet cosmonauts titled: "We Are Workers of the Same Army – The Army of Communism Builders":

> Soviet people–be it experienced specialists or young people at entry-level positions–together are bringing the future forward with their excellent work. Let the bright future of communism come sooner. Being aware of how valuable your work is, no matter how big or small, for your country and people, is most important in life.
>
> We are not yet famous for anything. The launch hour is still ahead. But each of us is always ready to perform any task set by the Party, by the people. Our current task is exploration of space routes, and we will do our best to perform it with flying colors. To do this, we have to work hard, train hard... study spaceships and how to control them, become experts in such fields of science and technology that we knew very little about before we enrolled as astronauts.
>
> We are attracted to space not only by curiosity. Space flights contribute to the development of science, discovery, and research of many secrets of nature. It's hard to tell how many answers to the questions pertinent to our physicists, doctors, chemists and biologists, metallurgists, and power engineers, are hidden in the boundless outer space. After all, from flight to flight, the task will be more and more difficult. Therefore,

1 Konstantin Tsiolkovsky (1857–1935) was famous not only for his engineering work. He worked consistently to develop the philosophy of cosmism and believed in the existence of extraterrestrial civilizations. His life was devoted to establishing a human connection with space.

2 D. Herrman, *Sky Explorers* (Mir, 1981), translated from German by K.B. Shingareva & A.A. Konopikhina.

3 Vladimir Ilyich Lenin, *Collected Works*, Volume 44, (Progress Publishing, 1970) 174.

4 *Printing in the RSFSR in 1922* (Gosizdat, 1922).

5 The Moscow branch of VKhUTEIN (Higher Artistic and Technical Institute) where Georgy Krutikov studied, was set up in 1926 on the basis of VKhUTEMAS (Higher State Artistic and Technical Workshops), formed as a result of the merger of two leading specialized educational institutions: the Stroganov Art and Industrial School and the Moscow School of Painting, Sculpture and Architecture.

6 VNIITE system had 10 regional branches that provided information, artistic and technical support, and guidance for design departments at 1,500 industrial enterprises throughout the country. VNIITE also set the vector for the development of design as a whole.

7 *Planet of Storms*, sci-fi feature film directed by Pavel Klushantsev (Leningrad Studio of Popular Science Films, USSR, 1961).

8 *Moscow-Cassiopeia*, sci-fi feature film directed by Richard Viktorov (Gorky Film Studio, USSR, 1973).

9 Nonconformism is an artistic movement that existed in the USSR in the 1960s–1980s. These artists refused to conform to socialist realism requirements. Many of them were persecuted by the state and were forced to leave USSR.

10 "Soviet Cosmonauts," *Technika Molodezhi Journal* no. 5 (1962), 3.

each of us, on the way to the launch pad, deeply believes that his work (yes, work!) makes our science, our people, even more powerful and brings forward the bright future to which all mankind will come – the communist future.[10]

Such statements were a vital part of Soviet communist propaganda. Astronauts became superheroes and space exploration became a national ideal. Astronauts were seen to personify the best qualities that a people should have. These idols of the generation not only called on their fellow Soviets to study and work; these words were supported by innumerable publications and film adaptations that sustained the illusion of a common desire for a brighter communist future.

The Soviet state imbued people's minds with speculations about space exploration, urging people to work and study hard to prepare for a vital mission of sharing communism with other earthbound peoples and extraterrestrial civilizations. These captivating aspirations were intended to leave little time for reflection on the real future of the Soviet state, its economy, and its society. Ideologically charged design, film, literature, and art diverted people's attention from the flaws of the government's policies, and from the censorship, repression, and low standard of living and work conditions in the USSR. The Soviet people were asked to dream of space and a bright communist future, in turn forgetting about the terrestrial hardships of their everyday.

Images from the Moscow Design Museum collection.

JAVIER ARPA FERNÁNDEZ

WHY?
WHY NOT?

Javier Arpa Fernández is the research and education coordinator of the Why Factory, curator of public programs in the Faculty of Architecture at TU Delft in The Netherlands, and Editor-in-Chief at MVRDV. He is author of *Paris Habitat: One Hundred Years of City, One Hundred Years of Life*, and a former deputy editor of Domus. In 2020, Arpa was appointed President of the French Architecture prize *d'A*.

✛ ARCHITECTURE, URBANISM, TECHNOLOGY

Earth is our home. It supports us and contains all known organic life in the universe. But this home is threatened from multiple sides. Anthropogenic climate disruption, uneven population growth, deforestation, pollution, and income disparity–to name just a few–are accelerating rapidly. These challenges demand action and imagination from all of us, from citizens to designers to policy makers.

In the face of these existential threats, how does design address rampant urbanization, overpopulation, catastrophe-driven migration, aggressive misogyny, white supremacism, imperialism, capitalist exploitation of the earth, or a takeover by artificial intelligence? For over a decade, the Why Factory at Delft University of Technology has been considering these issues as a means of advancing the fabrication of better architecture, better cities, and–by extension–a better planet. This work has spared no effort in revealing possibilities, repercussions, and potential limits of considering the organization of our world in different ways. The work is invested in finding modes and mediums to make better worlds.

The Why Factory is a research and education institute led by Professor Winy Maas at the Faculty of Architecture of Delft University of Technology. It was founded in 2008 and focuses on exploring possibilities for future cities through the production of models and visualizations. Education and research at the Why Factory are combined in a research lab and dissemination platform that aims to analyze, theorize, and construct future cities. The Why Factory investigates within the given world and produces scenarios beyond it. It proposes, constructs, and envisions hypothetical societies and cities. This design research produces observations, hypotheses, and statements in a visual and direct manner. The images produced are a combination of science and fiction, reflecting an approach that integrates systematic observations and the gathering of data with speculation and imagination through spatial and architectural means.

The Why Factory is inspired by works like Hieronymus Bosch's *The Garden of Earthly Delights*, which depicts a multitude of scenes that have led to a wide range of scholarly interpretations over the centuries. Whether the triptych's central panel is a moral warning, or a panorama of paradise lost is, we believe, up to a viewer's imagination and interpretation. What is for certain is that such a collection of scenes provokes amazement, reveals hidden patterns, and triggers new questions with each and every viewing.

In this spirit, the Why Factory operates through the positing of questions through the production of images and models. Can humanity make a planet that can cool down instead of warming up? Can we create new gardens of earthly delights by reforesting deserts and covering our cities in vegetation? Can we imagine a world with no hunger by changing agricultural methods? How do automation, nanomaterials, robotics, or biotechnology contribute to the production of healthier urban worlds? What might a planet of resilient cities created in the face of rising sea levels look like? What form does a planet take that is open and free? Can we imagine a planet without poverty or inequality?

The visions and models produced by the Why Factory are intended to incite astonishment and provoke wonder in the viewer. In them, one can see that what might begin as a fantasy in the imagination of the designer could, in fact, one day become a reality. To make these possibilities actionable in society–working across disciplinary boundaries and directly with policy makers–so as to let the imagination displayed in these visions materialize in the built environment is the driver of the Why Factory's work.

From this perspective, the position of the Why Factory is that it is necessary to doubt, dream, and imagine more. French surrealist poet Paul Éluard once wrote that "there is another world, and it is in this one." For the Why Factory, there are many worlds, they are all in this one, and they are all worthy of exploration.

1

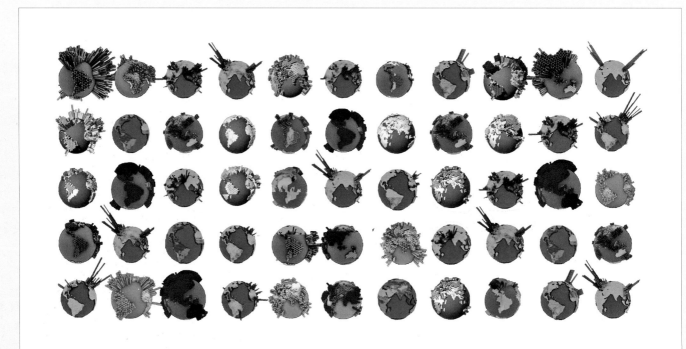

3

1 Planet Maker I

In collaboration with RMIT Melbourne and University of Technology Sydney

As the planet moves deeper into the Anthropocene, a shift of focus moves from the world of architecture to an architecture of the world. Here architecture has the potential to explore beyond its traditional disciplinary borders, the possibilities, repercussions, and limits of organizing the world in different ways. Considering spatially, as well as politically, how technology disruptions can change assumptions about the future of the world, Planet Maker endeavors to find ways to make better worlds. Rather than a top-down approach, Planet Maker seeks to become a tool of exploration and simulation where "what if's" are tested to give guidance and inspiration for future planet makers. Iteration, variation, and levels of intensity address the need to keep as many options as possible open for discussion with those who make the decisions affecting our daily lives.

2 Planet Maker II

In collaboration with RMIT Melbourne

Can we simulate possible scenarios that can change the planet? How might we script those future planet scenarios? What do we need to know to achieve this? Who are our key planet actors? How do we test their needs and capacities? How do we track the reaction of other actors to a single hypothesis? How do we identify the places that need close attention? Can we predict new planet thresholds based on conflict mapping? What kind of gaming system is needed? How do these planets look and why? How would these planetary scenarios affect the future of our cities?

3 Sky City

The futuristic transportation tunnels of Elon Musk snaking beneath cities like underground waterslides forming a high-speed public transportation system will soon be reality. The first flying cars are quickly becoming available on the commercial market. Commercial sub-orbital flights are just around the corner connecting New York and London in under half an hour. Sky City looks beyond these innovations to envision technologies that will allow for a truly new mobility around our planet. Is it really the monorail or hyperloop that will fundamentally transform mobility? Or can we look at it in a different way? While these huge infrastructure projects take up enormous amounts of land in our cities and hence the earth's habitable surface, it is time to think about the next step. What if we do not need any infrastructure? What if we can move up, down, left, right, or rotate in any direction at any time? What if we could fly?

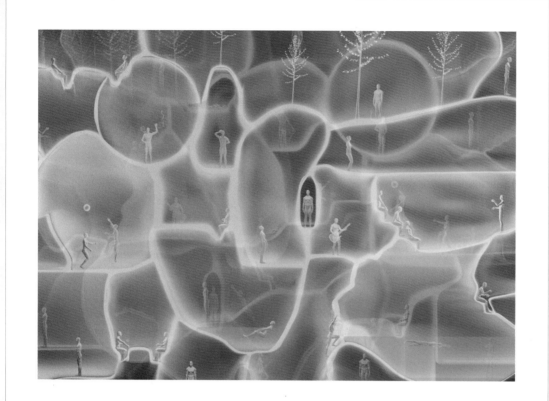

1

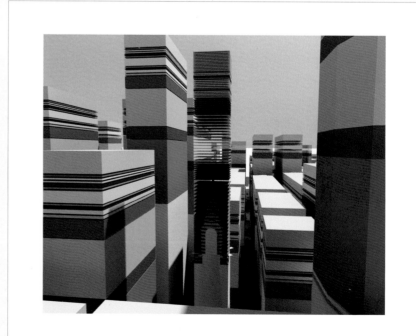

2

3

1 Barba

How might nanotechnology change buildings and cities in the future? Imagine a new substance that could be manipulated and altered in real time, a substance that is soft, bendable, and transformable. Imagine creating a flexible material that could change its shape, that could shrink and expand, that could do almost anything. Imagine that you could shape this material to form floors and walls, stairs and doors, and even furniture how and when you need it. Imagine that this material can be programmed to change its shape to your needs and desires at any moment of the day. The Why Factory calls this fictional material Barba. With Barba, we would be able to adapt our environment to every desire and to every need.

2 Food Print Manhattan

How much food do I consume? How much land is needed to grow it? Could we grow our food in the city? Could we feed all Manhattanites by growing food solely on Manhattan Island? Ideally the mouth of the consumer should be as close to the growing ingredients as possible, but can we achieve that? Foodprint Manhattan is a study on food consumption patterns and production capacities in Manhattan. It visualizes how much and what we consume and in turn the spatial consequences of that consumption. Foodprint Manhattan shows how more advanced food production methods compare to current production and how they could accelerate efficiency. The work puts current discussions about urban farming into context, by visualizing how much space is actually needed to produce our daily food.

3 Green Dip New York

The Green Dip is based on a software–the Green Maker–that calculates, among other parameters, the amount of carbon dioxide that could be captured by green cities. The Green Maker combines the knowledge of buildings with the knowledge of plants. A set of nine strategies can be chosen to dip any base urban typology in green. A catalogue of parametric elements allows for grasses, shrubs, and trees to be placed on any surface in, on, and around buildings. Knowledge of biomes ensures that only native plants can be used on sites. Green Dip digitally reimagines metropolises, like New York, and rethinks the typical set "green space," merging it with the existing urban fabric and transforming concrete jungles into green ones.

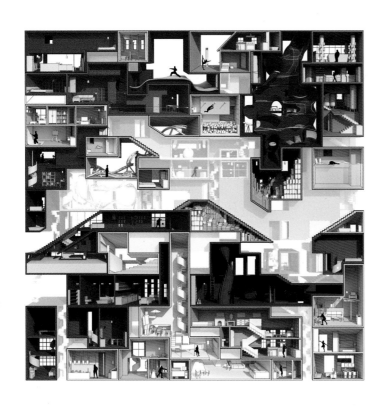

1

2

3

1 Wego

How do we make every dwelling become a desirable home? Wego investigates participatory processes applied to housing design. These processes establish a negotiation between the desires of each of the residents of a housing slab and help determine the design of their individual apartments. To achieve this, Wego manifests a particular interest in the development of a gaming process. This game leverages the specificities of each resident and transforms them into spatial needs. This way, unexpected housing typologies emerge within a truly human-driven housing architecture. The resulting intensity of the proposals is due to the convergence of many interests and the resolution of conflicts. We believe that this intensity, when applied to housing, can optimize land use, help combat inequality and counteract the centrifugal force condemning urban development to urban sprawl.

2 Biodivercity Lille

In a world where cities and urbanizations are increasingly occupying more and more surface area, the question of coexistence with animals and plants simultaneously becomes urgent and exciting. Biodivercity challenges the current mode of city-making based on pure artificiality. It develops new modes of urbanization that incorporate the life of animals and their natural habitat into our daily existence. These new city visions aim to highlight the value of biodiversity to levels never seen before—environmental, spatial, and economic benefits for all parties.

3 Maximum Venice

Drawn by its enchanting historic architecture and urban spaces, Venice today is suffocated by tourism. Its resident population dwindles year by year as cruise-trippers, Biennale-goers, and Airbnb-users take over the city. How much longer can this continue? How might we prevent one of Europe's greatest cities from being turned into a theme park? Could we take the existing buildings of Venice and simply make more of them? Maximum history, maximum density...Maximum Venice?

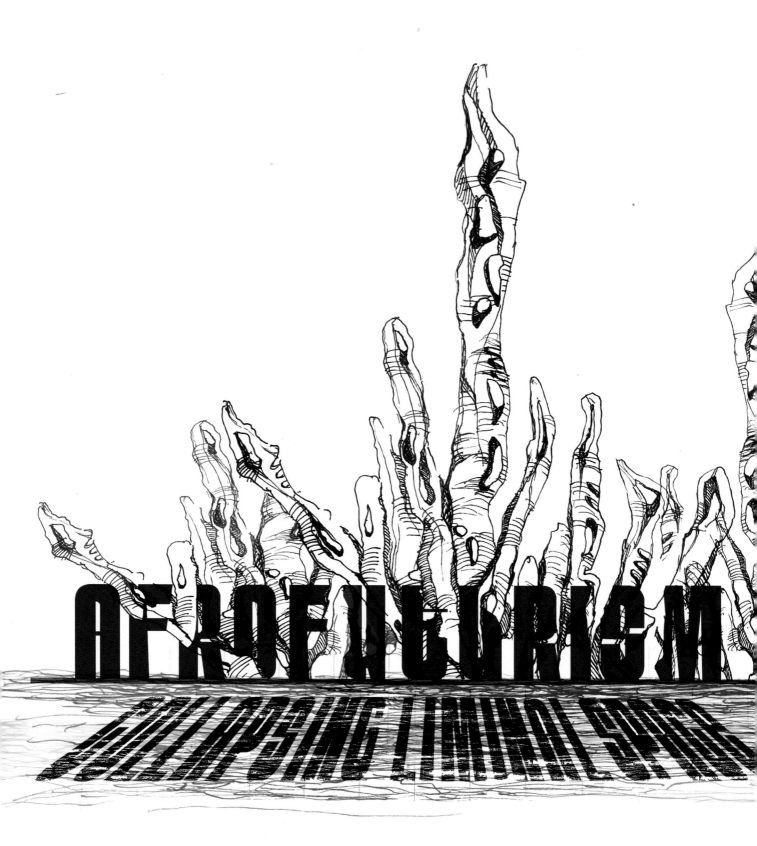

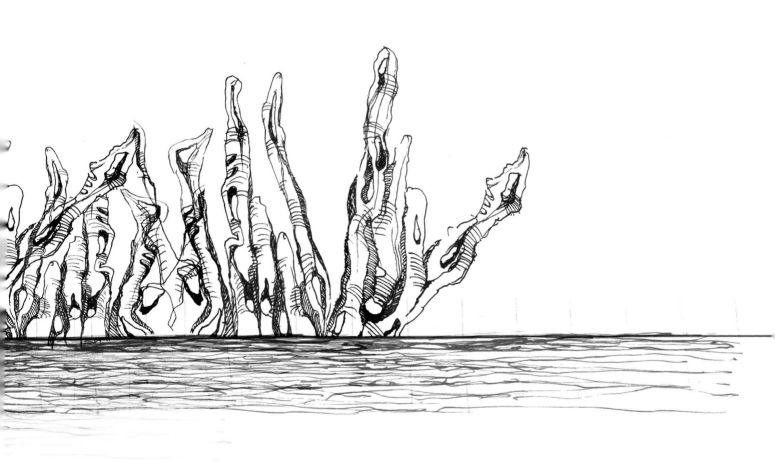

YTASHA L. WOMACK

Ytasha L. Womack is an author, filmmaker, independent scholar, dancer, and champion of the imagination. A leading Afrofuturist theorist and creator, she is author of *Afrofuturism: The World of Black Sci Fi & Fantasy Culture* (2013), which is widely taught in university curricula. She is co-curator of Carnegie Hall's Afrofuturism Festival and creates immersive Afrofuturist experiences inspired by her book *Rayla 2212* (2014). Her graphic novel *Blak Kube* (with Tanna Tucker) debuts in 2023.

✚ DIASPORIC STUDIES, AESTHETICS

While speaking at a feminism and technology conference in Montreal a few years back, I met a German artist who later visited me in Chicago. She wanted me to show her Afrofuturism. The weekend she arrived there weren't any Afrofuturism art events scheduled. Even if I'd found one, I had the impression that a festival or a gallery show wasn't really what she was looking for. Rather, she wanted me to take her to a physical space – a toppled Wiz head or an urban pyramid to the stars with young students coding; a Wakanda in the making with people in Funkadelic wear, bright and shiny in their new futures or resembling a Janelle Monae video. I had a tough time explaining to my guest that Afrofuturism as a lived experience, in my hometown at least, was not always in the form of a towering disco ball.

This isn't to say that in Chicago you won't find eager kids in cool outfits coding or chatting about quantum physics. It isn't to say that you won't see some colorful people in a shiny outfit or two. I wanted to take my guest to my friend's annual Debauchery Ball, an underground utopia for house music fans; or a bookstore with raucous afterhours discourse on futures; maybe a community tech incubator; or a church that had more sermons on the imagination, aspirationalism, and quantum mechanics than on Christian rhetoric. You see, Afrofuturism, in my experience, always hovers at the intersection of intention and protopia. It is a holding of a space where one can dream, be inspired, and actualize dreams, more than just a physical location of a particular activity. Afrofuturism doesn't always look like George Clinton's Spaceship that descended onto concert stages, although it may very well feel like that. Afrofuturism is a dynamism of histories and futures, often anchored in a space but not necessarily of the space. Yet, these activities are shapeshifting locales. They take place in spaces where the architecture is rarely designed for the energy it spawns. In my experience, Afrofuturism is as much the people in the space anchoring the experience as it is the extents of the space itself.

In retrospect, I've come of age in spaces—a historically Black college or a body positive dance school before body positivity existed—only to realize that I was in a utopia created by someone thinking to craft enriching places for people like me. People who walked this earth before me cultivated spaces where I'd cultivate a deeper sense of humanity, culture, and space/time. These spaces are normalized, sometimes appearing mundane, fluid when they weren't puzzling to casual onlookers who were expecting something other than what they witnessed. The nuance can go over one's head. If I took my colleague to either of these places–or to the church or the ball–would she be more confused? Would she end up looking for spaceship-inspired architecture and overt lectures on theory, rather than the ongoing transformation of the space through the multidimensional activity taking place within it?

Afrofuturism and the Liminal Space

Afrofuturism is a way of looking at the future and considering alternate realities through a Black cultural lens. It intersects the imagination, technology, liberation, mysticism, and Black cultures. It values the divine feminine, intuition, African and African diasporic wisdom systems, and time as nonlinear. It's an aesthetic that one can identify in music and film, but it's also a practice and method of thinking and inquiry. On several occasions I have given talks on Afrofuturism and dance to architecture students from the Saint-Etienne School of Architecture in France. Here, Xavier Wrona, a professor of architecture and organizer of the After the Revolution Conference, urges his students to utilize their architecture skills to address social issues where the answer is emphatically not the construction of a building. For example, in this work, dance is an interrogation of space that is both physical and rhythmic. Wrona's students are introduced to an array of ideas to reshape how they view the world. For me, this approach reinforces ideas I'd been contemplating through the lens of Afrofuturism – the idea of design as a way of thinking that has far-reaching implications beyond just what is physically constructed.

I think of spotting Afrofuturism in a place as using a particularly calibrated lens to see the wondrous world from another perspective. That is, seeing Afrofuturism is as much about how one engages with space and what one brings to the space, as it is about how the space itself is observed. Yet, an Afrofuturist space is its own kind of space. I often joke with a friend that the Harlem Renaissance was as much an outgrowth of Southern, Midwestern, and Caribbean creatives making Harlem their home and the intertwining their values as it was about 125th Street as a physical place – its design aesthetics and the politics of the times. From our perspective, it was the communalism of the time that energized the space. I would argue that Afrofuturist spaces are transcendent moments – sometimes brief, always sustained; sometimes extended, but always stretching across a timeline; reaching as far back as Ancient Egypt and as far forward as life beyond the galaxy to infuse energy into the now. Like other spaces of enchantment, Afrofuturism, in the Americas at least, hides in plain sight.

I conducted a workshop recently for a group of artists–many of whom were Afrofuturists–and in discussing how our imaginations worked, most said that they considered the imagination as an infinite realm of potential ideas. In this way, their task as creatives was to access this realm, and they did so by creating an emotional, mental, or sometimes physical space through which to download ideas from these inspired creations. What struck me about this conversation was the notion of creating a nonphysical space to access another nonphysical space in order to create something tangible. In thinking about Afrofuturism as space, the tangible work of, say, the space-fueled graphic novel or the time-racing costume, is just the tip of the iceberg of a larger synergy of philosophy. In that sense, Afrofuturism is as much the intangible space as it is the art that springs from this space. Here, I think of the jazz adage often credited to Miles Davis: "Pay attention to the notes I don't play." The in-betweens, the liminal space, is where the magic lies. This is a space that expands and contracts, it is a gateway to or the space of the Afrofuturist playground.

To Be Seen and Not Seen

Before jazz titan Sun Ra's rise to prominence, he walked the streets of 1950s Chicago as a little-known artist adorned with the Egyptian deity's solar disc and sparkling purple robes. "I just thought he was the cool guy who talked about spaceships and played at the Club Delisa," said film curator and Afrofuturist, Floyd Webb who used to spot Sun Ra in Washington Park. During that time, Sun Ra– born Herman Blount–would have been navigating through a dense neighborhood of old and new migrants whose newfound freedoms and subsequent segregation spawned an urbanicity that ran parallel with modernity. He would have been walking amongst and living in two- or three-story brownstones, some carved up to hold a dozen or more smaller units, or in the new two-story public housing placed at the neighborhood's southern border. He would have been able to walk to a lake as big as an ocean. The neighborhood's density quickened the exchange of ideas.

In one sense, someone dressed as Sun Ra would stand out among a population whose daily wear was typically populated with hats and two-piece suits. But Sun Ra, as unique as he was, was not an anomaly. Many people at that time talked of new futures, standing on literal soap boxes as they passed out literature to new Black residents with new freedoms and Southern roots. He was a part of a synergy of new Chicagoans interrogating possibility and identity. While Sun Ra was more obvious to the passing strangers who didn't know Bronzeville neighborhood edicts, he was a vibrant flower springing forth from a larger scene that included people adorned with Moorish-inspired garb from the previous century. But where was this scene actually located? If I raced back in time to show my German colleague Afrofuturism, would I take her to Washington Park? Or would the after-hours talks between musicians and patrons of like mind–the kind of scene that inspired the 1950s short film *Cry of Jazz*–be a better proximation of an Afrofuturist space?

Cry of Jazz was the first to film to declare that jazz as an artform was dead. This film by Edward Bland, scored by Sun Ra, declared that jazz–an intersection of fixed measures and improvisation–mirrored Black American life in Jim Crow America. As racial dynamics changed, the form of the music changed along with it. Although Bland was identifying the parallels between society and the nation's first original music form, he was also making a commentary on how one navigated space. Afrofuturist spaces nurture and make way for the mastery of improvisation. Yet, for as much as Sun Ra is heralded today,

I'm fascinated by how many devout music lovers had never actually heard of him when he was alive. Even for some who saw him, his lack of context rendered him and his significance nearly invisible.

This functioning in the liminal spaces is a defense mechanism; a method of safeguarding spaces. However, the situating of the liminal space is also a result of a Westernized lens that wrestles with seeing beyond the binary. This is why, I believe, so many people saw Sun Ra and simultaneously didn't see him at all. This could also account for me showing someone like my German friend an Afrofuturist space and being told that it is not Afrofuturist enough!

A Crossroads

AfriCOBRA, a Chicago-based art collective founded in the late 1960s was formed to create an aesthetic that highlighted Black life, bridged the Diaspora, and addressed social ills. Emerging from the creation of The Wall of Pride, a major mural project on Chicago's Southside in 1969, the collective would go on to embrace Kool-Aid colors–an array of mediums and mosaic textures that spoke to the new urban temperament and Black identity that came to be defined as the Black Arts Movement. Gerald Williams, one of the art collective's founding members, once said that the key aesthetic principle binding the group was the "mimesis at midpoint." This is the point in space where the real and the unreal, the objective and the nonobjective, the plus and the minus, meet. This is a point that is said to exist exactly between absolute abstraction and absolute realism.[1] Thinking of the proliferation of the crossroads–whether one is talking about blues music, Haitian Voudon, the Ancient Egyptian Anhk, the points on the Congolese Cosmogram, the intersection of where the sky meets the earth, or where the unseen world interacts with the seen world–is an ever-present aesthetic concern in African diasporic art, philosophy, and space. I think of this framing of intersections between worlds as one that particularly speaks to how I personally experience Afrofuturism and read its aesthetic in various cities around the world.

Afrofuturism has another intersection; it is a crossroads in which the cultures within the African diaspora and continent meet. As an American descendent of people scattered across

North and South America during the transatlantic slave trade and the struggles that came afterward, I've always been aware of the fragmentation of Black cultures and the intentional recovery process. This is a practice akin to quilt making or remixing in hip hop in that it requires a reconnection with memories both lost and reactivated. Here, numerous cities populated with Black residents across the continent honed their own survival and thriving practices, reworking or preserving specific strains of an African philosophy that is clearly evident in how people congregate, their rituals, their art, their music, and the particular ways they use space. Thinking on the "data thief" character in John Akomfrah's 1996 film *The Last Angel of History*, I too sometimes feel as if I'm trekking from city to city, gathering vestiges of philosophies honed in these contexts.

For example, some years back I spoke at the Ashe Cultural Center in New Orleans where the musician and Congo Square Preservation Society founder Luther Gray served as my tour guide. In preparing for my talk, I asked Gray what aspect of Afrofuturism I should emphasize in my presentation. I was aware that New Orleans Black and Creole residents were very connected to African mysticism and the realm of the imagination. In the face of relentless catastrophic hurricanes and repeated racist attempts at erasure, this preservation of African and Indigenous culture was both a form of empowerment and a form of resistance. While the architecture of New Orleans is often French colonial, the adornments, the art, and temperament of the city are emphatically not. The open cultural practices, from the second line to the music battles of the Mardi Gras Indians, are a clear form of liberation. The rechurning of these practices creates a sense of timelessness in the city. The popular saying that New Orleans is a French City with an African soul takes on new meaning. Nevertheless, while the history, liberation, mysticism, and imagination were a big part of the culture of New Orleans, thinking on how to envision a future that didn't disavow that culture was a genuine challenge. In New Orleans, what I often experienced as the liminal in Chicago was quite present and woven into the essential character of the Crescent City's culture – as if the liminal was a blanket on New Orleans; a junction where the seen and unseen comingle.

In contrast, Chicago is a city whose residents are seemingly always assessing their particular identity and their progress as a measure of this identity. A New York-based friend once joked that Black Chicagoans are hosting panels on identity more frequently than any other place he knows – a fact I really can't argue against. He noted that Chicago's Black residents are constantly asking: "Where am I now?" or "How much access do I have?" or "Am I successful?" These questions are the offshoot of being descendants of the Great Migration and more recent moves to the city in the hope of achieving something here that they couldn't achieve in the spaces where their families hailed from. This line of questioning puts the future and the frustrations with never quite being there in constant dialogue. Liberation is future forward but can sometimes feel like a hamster wheel with the constant effort necessary to keep up and bring history and wisdom systems along with you. Yet, there's more grounding in Black history in Chicago than in many other American cities. Here, knowing history is viewed as essential to moving forward; a Sankofa idea of bringing the best into the future. But that history is tied in the making of the modern and the evolution into the postmodern. In Chicago, Afrofuturism can feel like a grinding response to postmodernism. On the contrary, in a city as old as New Orleans, where enslaved Africans once lived, Afrofuturism is experienced as the root.

Whereas Black Chicago hops in and out of the liminal space and New Orleans hovers at the crossroads, my experience in Dakar, Senegal, demonstrates the expansiveness of what I think of as "the in-between." It was in Dakar that I realized that my experience of the in-between was really a space where the African relationship to the subconscious and its machinations was most valued. In Dakar, there is a symmetry between the food, the architecture, the fashion, the culture, the wisdom systems, and the art without the tensions that I often experience in American cities. In the US, being comfortable with one's body can be an inherent tension. In Dakar, I didn't have to explain an African relationship to time, space, and a future because it was instinctively understood and reinforced through the given culture, beliefs, and environment. Dakar is often romanticized, and justifiably so. But I credit the poetic symmetry in the aesthetic in part to

1 Jeffreen M. Hayes (ed.), *AfriCobra: Messages to the People* (Museum of Contemporary Art, North Miami and Gregory R. Miller & Co., 2021), 52.

2 The Senegalese-American artist and entrepreneur Akon recently announced plans to develop a city of the future in Senegal. Early reports tout this endeavor as a luxury city fueled by clean energy and built on cryptocurrency. Billed as a "home back home" for people of the African diaspora, "Akoncity" is said to welcome people from around the world. The drawings are stunning, highlighted by amoeba-like buildings with broad implications of new technologies.

the fact that Senegal's first president was actually a poet. Being a coastal city, Dakar has had a comfortable symbiotic relationship with cultural influences, musically embracing Nigerian and American hip hop, breakdancing, and Brazilian capoeira alongside Angolan kizomba, while still championing Mbalax. While there are tensions around new developments and the interest of investors,[2] one's relationship to a future isn't yet abstracted.

I was in Dakar as part of the Black Rock Senegal residency created by renowned artist Kehinde Wiley, and it was during this visit that I first experienced the epic *Door of Return* – a monument constructed on the coast in Yoff as a commemoration of the "Door of No Return" where thousands of Africans were enslaved and sold to distant lands. I would argue that this highly charged construct is in fact a kind of Afrofuturist space. The assemblage of artists and creatives who come through its frame pondering identity and futures are actively looking to the culture of Dakar to inform their work. A space of aspiration and grandeur, the *Door of Return* infuses Dakar's postmodern architecture, using the sunlight, the beach's large black rocks, and the Atlantic as fundamental design elements.

Although I can point to other buildings that speak to a future, I still find myself centralizing the intentions of these spaces. If I brought my German colleague to Dakar's coast with its array of surfers and fishermen or to a dance battle nearby and said "this is Afrofuturism," I think she'd still look at me with a hint of confusion. Any architecture that's created as Afrofuturist has to be anchored in the stream of culture as widening or collapsing the in-betweens permeating with African/African diasporic philosophical thought. Any building that takes on the Afrofuturist aesthetic must be understood as a wave in the bigger ocean.

Opposite: "The Door of No Return" on Gorée Island, Senegal, which thousands of enslaved Africans passed through on their forced journeys to distant lands.

IN CONVERSATION WITH
ALEXANDRA DAISY GINSBERG

Alexandra Daisy Ginsberg is a globally recognized artist based in London. Formally trained in architecture and design interactions, she holds a PhD from the Royal College of Art. Ginsberg's artwork, writing, and curatorial practices engage humanity's increasingly fraught relationship with nature and technology. Specifically, the increasingly designed intersections and interactions between so-called nature and emerging technologies. Her work has been exhibited at MoMA in New York, the Centre Pompidou in Paris, and the Royal Academy in London. Coincidentally, having once considered landscape architecture as a career, her most recent work, for the Eden Project in Cornwall, is a garden. **Javier Arpa Fernandez + Christopher Marcinkoski** spoke to Ginsberg for LA+.

+ To begin in an obvious place, can you speak to your relationship to the term speculation and speculative design?

I find the multiple meanings of the word "speculation" in the context of design both interesting and problematic. What we think it means can get lost in translation outside the very small field of speculative design. Outside of design, the word "speculation" is often associated with financial speculation, which when used with "design" can be interpreted as a desire to materialize a future rather than question it. Even within mainstream design, the term gets conflated with more commercial ideas of "doing work on spec" – in other words, for free. Back in 2010 I told someone I was a speculative designer and they joked, "Oh, so you *want* to be a designer?"

I did my master's at the Royal College of Art between 2007 and 2009 in Design Interactions–a department led by Anthony (Tony) Dunne and Fiona Raby, and Tony later co-supervised my PhD. Design Interactions is associated with developing speculative design methods, which have since spread widely in many different directions. But in my own artistic practice, I'm interested in the methods Tony and Fiona were pursuing, with speculation grounded in a critical framework and used as a tool to question. Their approach had roots in the critical Italian Radical Design movement of the 1960s. I see this as different to related practices like design fiction, often used in more commercial settings, where there is a closer link to financial speculation and futures; there, speculative designs are used to create stories to bet on a future or find a particular path to a future to invest in. But despite these different motivations, the two are often described together as single practice.

In Design Interactions, we were experimentally using design as a tool to explore the social, cultural, and ethical implications of emerging technologies. There's been a valid questioning of how critical it can be, given the elitist subject matter of the work and who it is done by, and that it's often encountered as a gallery practice. *What is speculative design for? Who is it for? Who is consulted? Whose stories are told? Who is the audience? Who benefits?* There's a lot to unpack as there are nuances to each project that emerge from a research practice, and generalization isn't necessarily useful. Often my primary audience was the scientific community and each artwork was created with that audience in mind, responding to synthetic biology research and the field's narratives; then they ended up in gallery spaces. But of course, I was practicing in a privileged space as a privileged person, and the issues I was exploring were much larger than the space I was working from and the knowledge I was drawing on.

Moving away from the term "speculation" itself and to its intentions, in my PhD, I looked at Foucault's idea of heterotopia and my idea of "critical imaginaries." I wanted to create spaces of imagination that were less about the implications of new technologies, which easily tends towards locating fictions in the future, and instead think about creating spaces where we can reflect back on the world today and the decisions being made now. Heterotopias are places that are other–not better or worse, like utopias or dystopias–but different. These spaces can be parallel worlds, in the future, in the past, or nowhere in particular. The body of work I have made since plays with these ideas of other and reflection.

With my latest commission for the Eden Project in Cornwall, UK, I am in some ways coming back to an earlier dream of being a landscape architect. *Pollinator Pathmaker* (2021–) is an artwork for pollinators, not for humans. As an artwork, it is more practical than my earlier speculative works – I have created an algorithm that designs planting schemes to maximize pollinator diversity, rather than maximize human aesthetic joy – but *Pollinator Pathmaker* also makes us ask what or who do we design for? It's questioning whether art can be useful; if it isn't in the gallery, what or who is it for? If I'm making art about the ecological crisis, what am I asking the audience to do? How can I offer agency, not just despair?

+ Do you see your work as being an agent of change?

Because my training was in architecture and in Design Interactions, not fine art, there's always a question of solutionism hanging over my head. Can design be anything other than a discipline to solve problems? Can I avoid trying to solve problems? My PhD looked at how design as a practice of bettering–a process of changing an existing situation to a preferred or better one, to paraphrase Herbert Simon–leads to an assumption that design makes things *better*. But design is very context dependent. What is better in that context, whose idea of better is being realized, and who gets to decide? Most design today is operating under the influence of capitalism, and so the focus of design is on extraction and producing things to sell. But I'm curious about different kinds of design. Now I'm asking whether we can design for other species without human benefit. Is it possible for design to be altruistic or is design as a human activity exclusively serving our own self-interest? Are we inevitably focused on bettering for ourselves? "Bettering" nature, the environment that we are part of, ultimately serves our own interests.

My work with synthetic biology in the first 10 years of my practice meant embedding myself within a new field of technoscience to reflect what was going on within it – a way to pick up weak signals of the future and reflect on what was being proposed. But rather than asking an audience to pick a future–*Is this one good or bad?*–I wanted to make work that would have an impact on the present – enabling us to change in the present because that is where change happens; the present is where the futures we end up with are chosen. In the same way there is no one single future, there is no one single present. We are all experiencing different versions of a present from our different circumstances and positions. Rather than making a single vantage point to look at the future and choose one future from many, can you create a place to reflect back on multiple presents and, in turn, empower people to act now? It's semantics, but for me that perspectival shift helps.

Following that line of thinking, much of my work in synthetic biology was aimed at synthetic biologists, rather than the general public: *I hear you saying this, it leads me to this idea, here is a way to represent that, what is your response?* – using the creation of a design object as an instrument of discourse. I think my work as an "agent of change" (if at all) was that approach.

My four works from 2019–*Resurrecting the Sublime; The Substitute; The Wilding of Mars; and Machine Auguries*–use technology as a vehicle to question our relationship with the natural world. These works were meant for the gallery space, which is problematic in its own way. It forced me to consider what I'm asking the audience to do with the work? The pieces were intended to elicit an emotion of loss, but if they are not directed at a specialist community that has the ability to actually enact change, what is the audience's agency? There was a review of the *Eco-Visionaries* exhibition at London's Royal Academy of Arts (2019), which showed works by artists and designers responding to the planetary ecological emergency. It singled out *The Substitute* and said something to the effect of: "Ginsberg offers no answers." I loved that. Why would we assume that artists or designers should or *could* have solutions to something as complex as this?

+ You've talked a bit about time, and the intention of your work to not actually be about the future but instead the present, but we wonder if you could say a bit about scale? So much of your work uses elements that are somehow immediately tangible to an audience–the plant, the rhino, the bird–as a means of engaging with or framing questions around larger systems.

That really comes from my Design Interactions training and the idea that you can take a familiar object and build a whole world around it to tell stories. That struck me in contrast to architecture–both from studying it and teaching it–where the goal often seems to be volume of production and comprehensive description at every scale. The Design Interactions critical design approach advocated for focused elaboration of one tangible thing, an object–from the future or the present, this world or another–and then to allude to how people might interact with that thing. The strange familiarity of interacting with a thing, even a new thing, allows people to connect with the story. The other aspect–and this is really when I became engaged with synthetic biology–was back in early 2008 my friend and collaborator Sascha Pohflepp heard a talk by the synthetic biologist Drew Endy and told me, "Daisy, you're going to find this amazing–these engineers want to *design* biology." That began my deep dive into the field.

I thought, "So, engineers are going to design biology using DNA as code, using it as a programming language–that's unbelievable!" And if biology is going to become a design material, what is going to be designed, what is good design, and who will decide? If you're thinking in this way, you can see the plant or rhino as design objects. Then how are these "things" any different than a phone or other everyday things we use? *Growth Assembly* (2009, with Sascha Pohflepp) ends up being a story of a response to an environmental crisis where synthetic biology has been pushed forward to the point where plants are designed, engineered, to grow useful objects. Everything is told minimally through a set of botanical drawings, setting up a world for the viewer to imagine themselves.

+ Your PhD dealt with the notion of *better*. Can you say a bit about what motivated that work? And perhaps to what degree those questions remain within your current work?

My PhD asked, "What is better?" People want the answer, and it's impossible to give one as there isn't "one" better. We have to do the work to discuss together what we want to be better, what are the shared values we advocate for, down to the actions that can lead us there. That said, my idea of better is to protect our shared environment. I find it hard to see anything else as the primary goal, but that is a luxury given my privileged circumstances—I have the luxury of being able to worry about my recycling, my carbon footprint, and the future. But if your primary concern is the present—of putting food on the table—the long-term future of humanity is less important. And my daily actions don't align with my definition of better: I travel, I consume; what's better for me in the short term differs wildly from my long-term view. But if we circle back, if there is an ethics of better defined by a common good, should that be a long-term or short-term common good? What is our duty as a species, how do we balance individual needs and planetary needs in a common good? It all becomes very messy, very quickly.

Working in synthetic biology—which led me to my PhD—I was left in the position of not knowing what my role was anymore. I was surrounded by people who wanted to make the world better, developing a technology shaped by their individual beliefs of what was better. I started off as a kind of critical agent of subterfuge, creating a space for artists and designers within synthetic biology but after ten years I had to ask, "Where am I? Have I become the poster-girl for synthetic biology – effectively promoting it?" To be critical about synthetic biology, I first had to explain to people what synthetic biology was and what it promised, and was essentially promulgating it, which became problematic for me.

The funding for my work was often from government agencies that had identified a bit of budget for artists to make work about the science being produced described as public engagement but really was about encouraging public acceptance. You can't, then, make very critical work because it could burn bridges with the field or its funders, so it became a conflicted space for me.

+ Can you elaborate on what you mean by "conflicted space?"

I wrote in my PhD about trouble; constantly finding myself in difficult situations. I was *other* to the field: I was not a synthetic biologist but was working with synthetic biologists in their space, excited by their work, but questioning it. I was working in uncomfortable ways. Donna Haraway's *Staying with the Trouble*[1] echoed for me, because I felt like I was constantly troubling things, making trouble, finding myself in trouble, because what I was doing was based on conflict: creating dialogue from my position as not being part of the field. I was reacting to what I was learning and hearing. But my biggest conflict I realized was about being in rooms full of people promising they can make the world better.

When I spoke at TEDglobal in 2011 about my work in synthetic biology, it didn't go well—I was told I had too many questions and not enough answers. I was trying to be critical, but also optimistic. I felt that they wanted me to talk about how synthetic biology could make the world a better place. But I couldn't offer

Opposite: "Herbicide Gourd" illustration by Siôn Ap Tomas from *Growth Assembly* (2009) by Daisy Ginsberg and Sascha Pohflepp.

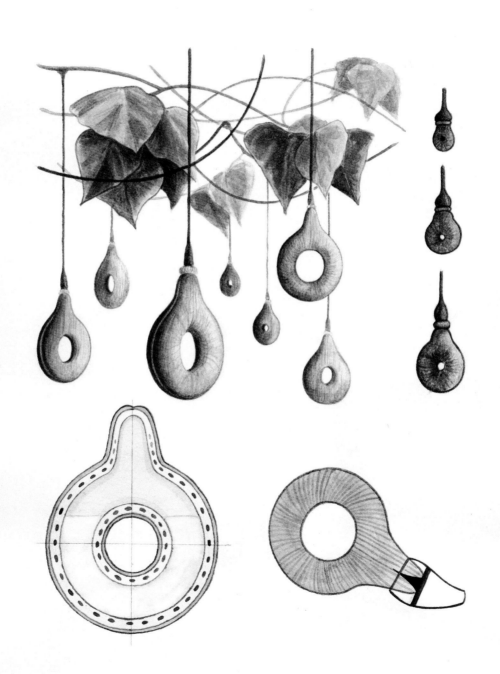

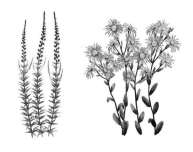

a clear message, all I had was a feeling that art and design could ask critical questions of a field that promised it could make the world a better place, and that, to me, mattered.

I realized that every conference I attended, whether in technology or design, was about this promise of making the world better through whatever it was the person was doing. I started to think: What is better? And whose better? And who is deciding? I began to track all of these uses of the term better from advertising to politics and realized then it didn't have any single meaning. This was the conflict central to my PhD. As I explored where ideas of progress and the common good align with better, I realized that better is a word that we assume contains the values of progress, an uplifting of all humanity through science and knowledge. But progress excludes the environment we live in; it's a product of Enlightenment thinking that is about emancipation from the natural world. Or we assume that when a "better world" is invoked, it means serving the common good, but better is tied up in economic and political contexts, which have other needs and values.

I started exploring how design relates to better. And here I think of Herbert Simon's idea of changing an existing situation to a preferred one, because there is a very clear route to better – *If I am cold, I can put a blanket on, I will be better if I have a blanket, I can make a blanket*. But what we think of as design today is caught up in the capitalist system. Design as we know it is a product of the Industrial Revolution, with a focus on differentiation – differentiating one plate from the plate of a different manufacturer. I looked for examples where design operates outside of that, where the focus was solving versus selling, and there are examples of course, both contemporary and historical.

In synthetic biology, I found three broad churches of *better*. Specifically, I was looking at how dreams of better held by a visionary could be disseminated and how those visionaries bring people on board, and how those visions result in very different kinds of designed things and potential futures. The first was the vision of Drew Endy, of an open-source DNA parts "library" where sequences of DNA information are available for free but the inventions that they are combined into are patentable, which he envisions could lead to a more collaborative version of the future. Then there is the industrial vision that ties the economy to the environment and simply replaces what we already use – jet fuel from ancient biological matter (fossil fuel), for example, with jet fuel engineered from recently living biological matter (sugarcane). Not changing what we do, just what we use to do it. That's a vision where better means the same economic system, just via biology.

And finally, the third faction—which interests me most—is the camp of bettering nature – bringing mammoths back or engineering gene drives. Making nature less harmful by, say, eliminating mosquitos; or, the extreme version, by bettering (read: engineering) humans – further emancipating ourselves from the natural world in a very modernist way. Reflecting on these different visions led to the formulation of a model for myself, embracing heterotopias and critical imaginaries rather than better futures.

My real interest is the exploitation of the natural world. Why do we do this as humans? What is this desire to manipulate and design and control our environment? And if we really are this amazing species with imagination and the ability to think about the future, why are we so bad at preserving that future for future generations? Why do we have long-term aspirations, but only short-term abilities? Of course, much of that has to do with political systems and the power that one system holds over the structuring of society. Really, the answer to the question, "What is better" is that it depends on who we are in that moment, and drilling down into who "we" is.

+ There is obviously a sort of modulation of the dystopian in your work, yet there are also traces of what might be characterized as a kind of optimism. These two aspects seem to offer a productive tension for you, but they also make us wonder how optimistic or pessimistic you are?

Better links to the human ability to hope. Richard Howells describes creativity as a utopian impulse – you have to believe things could be better to create. That said, I'm very pessimistic about what we are doing to our planet. The world will continue, but ecologically it won't be "better."

I attended a conference in 2013–which is summed up in a fascinating book called *Strange Natures*[2] by Kent Redford and Bill Adams–that was the first formal meeting of the synthetic biology community and the conservation community. *Designing for the Sixth Extinction* (2013–2015) was my response to the conference, where I was exposed for the first time to discussions of engineering coral to withstand warmer waters or using synthetic biology to try to eliminate avian malaria. That is, intentionally releasing things into the wild to fix problems in nature. This brings up one of the most profound questions about synthetic biology which is, how is it possible to make the decision to permanently affect nature? If you infect nature to save it, does "nature" still exist? What do we value, how do we preserve it, and are preservation or conservation even useful ideas to hold on to when it comes to nature and ecosystems and biology, which are always changing and evolving and are not static? How do we then think about design, which we understand as a static practice that makes artifacts, in relation to something so fluid and changing? Asking the question just opens up more questions!

+ There is a very legible arc in your work, both in terms of subject matter and scale. However, one project stands out as being incongruous with the rest – that is, your work about Mars. Can you talk about that work and how you see it fitting into some of the things you have mentioned thus far?

Well, let me begin by saying I have no intention of leaving Earth. I solidly belong here. *The Wilding of Mars* (2019) addressed two problems for me. One, I was interested in creating a heterotopia and in spatial landscape practice as a way to do that, having read Jorge Luis Borges's *The Garden of Forking Paths*. His short story describes a garden situated in time, not space, where you could get to the same point in time... there are many parallel worlds in progress, but they eventually rejoin in some way. This idea is reflected in evolution in things like eyes. Octopi have eyes, we have eyes; we are not related to them, eyes have evolved separately in response to things like climatic conditions, physics, the way that the Earth is – eyes become a solution to the problem of being on Earth. I wanted to explore parallel worlds shaped by the circumstances of the environment.

This riffs on my favorite science experiment, by Richard Lenski at Michigan State. He has been conducting a long-term evolutionary experiment since the 1980s, tracking

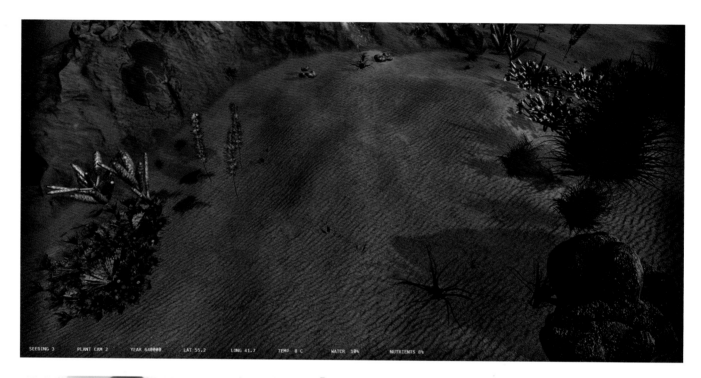

SEEDING 3   PLANT CAM 2   YEAR 640000   LAT 55.2   LONG 41.7   TEMP 8 C   WATER 10%   NUTRIENTS 8%

12 parallel populations of *E. coli* that all started from the same population. I find it a wonderful example of a garden of forking paths in reality. The populations exhibit similarities due to their identical world conditions, but they also diverge. I wanted to create a garden that exists in time and space, with multiple parallel worlds.

In *The Wilding of Mars*, there are always two parallel worlds unfolding from the same starting point. The simulation of plant life evolving on Mars, away from human influence, was created by running an evolutionary simulation over a million years twice; different things emerge under each simulation. The conditions on Mars at the beginning are similar, but they diverge. The intention is that the viewer reflects on those divergences and begins making value judgements—"I like that one better" or "I prefer this here"—but, then, the question is *why*? I want people to reflect on that.

The second problem was the brief. I was asked to propose a work for a show called *Moving to Mars* at the Design Museum in London. I was concerned since the exhibition was about colonizing Mars. How is it okay to talk about colonization of another planet when colonialism hasn't exactly worked out well for so many people and so many species here on this one! Somehow the word "colonize" is neutralized when it comes to this particular alien territory. Also, it's deeply problematic that Mars is widely presented as a backup planet when it is a terrible, terrible hostile place for Earth life. And it may have its own indigenous life – what right do we have? I was told it was meant to be a family show, so I could be critical, but I had to be optimistic. I thought that was an amazing provocation!

I had read a paper titled "Designing Autonomy: Opportunities for New Wildness in the Anthropocene" that speculates on the benefits of designing an algorithm to maintain wilderness space and how that algorithm could be a better curator than any human. My immediate thought was, well surely the algorithm will just keep humans out or attempt to kill them off? But I found it really interesting as a provocation, and it led me to the idea of wilding Mars. This immediately sets up a whole raft of problems: which species, who goes? It's still a violent project, but it also sets up the question of altruism. Could we tolerate not possessing Mars and instead turn it into a repository of life while we sort out our situation here on Earth? I wanted it to be a counterargument to the show; a means of using beauty and the aesthetics of a colonial landscape painting to insidiously test that proposition. It was an experiment in creating a heterotopia, and a gentle way for me to declare my absolute distaste for Mars colonization.

+ You have mentioned the idea of operating as an "other" and talked about your work both in terms of design and as an artist. We're curious how much disciplinary identity matters in your work. And to what extent does operating as an artist versus operating as a designer change the nature of your work?

I came from architecture, I went into a design master's program, and then spent a lot of time in synthetic biology calling myself a designer. It was a useful way to get into that field because the social contract between art and design is different; the designer is seen as a service provider. In art-science collaborations, maybe you are given a bench in a lab and the presumption is that the artist is going to make something interesting over there, but as a designer, there was a lot of confusion as to what I was there for as it was new. I was offering my own version, making up the role as I went along. I was asking, "what is the role of design in synthetic biology?"

But over time, I realized I was making art about design about synthetic biology! I see my work as art, but it doesn't really matter. It comes back to capitalism in that these two worlds of art and design are split and that you are forced to choose one; both operate in their own financial world. If I say that I'm an artist, the conversation continues – it's understood that I'm doing my thing. If I say I am designer, then the interrogation begins. Are you a fashion designer? No. A graphic designer? Well, no. An architectural designer? No, well you see I worked in synthetic biology for 10 years and now...

+ The reason we ask about discipline is less about the labels and more about this question of values. As in, whose values? That is, different disciplines value different things. Even within different camps of scientific inquiry, there are different value sets that get privileged depending on the subject area.

I would agree with that and calling myself an artist allows me to short circuit a lot of those questions. Whereas before it was useful to be a designer to make the work be disruptive in the way that I wanted it to. Now that's no longer necessary for what I'm doing.

I like the design field. It's a friendly place! I left the practice of architecture because I found it a difficult culture. I love teaching architecture because my students aren't actually doing architecture, but thinking between scales. Those skills remain with me and are obvious within my work. But now, my main interest is what do I want to do, and how am I going to achieve it?

+ Can you tell us a bit more about your work with the Eden Project?

I am interested in designing for other species and asking whether that's even possible. As I touched on earlier, for *Pollinator Pathmaker* I developed an algorithm that maximizes empathy for other species. Developing *Pollinator Pathmaker* has meant working with an amazing team from horticulturalists at Eden, to a string theory physicist, web developers, researchers, and pollination experts, to ask, "If pollinators designed gardens, what would humans see?"

The algorithm works with a curated plant palette – a database of plants that have each been chosen for their specific pollinators, from bees to moths to wasps to beetles, and ensures blooming throughout the year. The algorithm solves for empathy, which I defined as creating planting schemes that always serve the most pollinator species possible, offering the most forage for the broadest number of species. Through patterning of the garden, ease of foraging is also optimized. The algorithm designs for the way different insects fly – bees, for example, memorize traplines, optimized routes that solve for the shortest distance between flowers they visit.

That is actually a very complex mathematical problem called "the traveling salesman problem," which concerns finding the shortest distance between the maximum number of points within a period. The result is a network of circuits or doughnuts, embedded in the planting pattern; it is a garden that probably no human would ever design. The horticulturalists were originally slightly horrified because there is no aesthetically unified palette or layering of form and texture. You have all flower colors, all shapes, all sizes, jumbled up together in service of pollinators' tastes, not people's tastes. We've planted the first "Edition Garden" at the Eden Project in Cornwall – a 55 m2 garden that will formally open in May 2022. The next will be planted in Hyde Park,

1 Donna Haraway, *Staying with the Trouble: Making Kin in the Chthulucene* (Duke University Press, 2016).

2 Kent Redford & Bill Adams, *Strange Natures: Conservation in the Era of Synthetic* Biology (Yale University Press, 2021).

3 Bradley Cantrell, Laura Martin & Erle C. Ellis, "Designing Autonomy: Opportunities for New Wildness in the Anthropocene," *Trends in Ecology and Evolution* 32, no. 3 (2017): 156–66.

4 https://pollinator.art/.

London, commissioned by the Serpentine Gallery; then later in 2022, we'll plant our first international Edition Garden, in Berlin, with a new plant list for the Berlin region. Each of these gardens is part of an unlimited edition: the more individual artworks for pollinators we plant, the greater the value of the whole network.

The second part of the project is an interactive website[4] where anyone can create their own edition of the artwork, just by entering their garden conditions, and playing with the algorithm. You can fly through a visualization of the garden—a 3-D composite of my paintings of each flower—and if you like it, download the planting instructions and plant it. The idea is a distributed fabrication model for an artwork. Big Edition Gardens spark off local networks of DIY Edition Gardens, combining together into our ambition to make the world's largest climate positive artwork. We're using art to give agency and hope. *Pollinator Pathmaker* won't solve the pollinator crisis, but it brings attention to why we plant, what we plant, who it's for, and who gets to plant. How do we see the world with empathy? How do we see the world through other eyes? It's a big complex project but the challenge is very fun.

Above: "Self-inflating Antipathogenic Membrane Pump" from *Designing for the Sixth Extinction* (2013-2015) by Alexandra Daisy Ginsberg.

Previous top: *The Wilding of Mars* (2019) by Alexandra Daisy Ginsberg.

Previous bottom: "The *E. chromi* Scatalog" from *E. chromi* (2009) by Alexandra Daisy Ginsberg and James King with the University of Cambridge 2009 iGEM team.

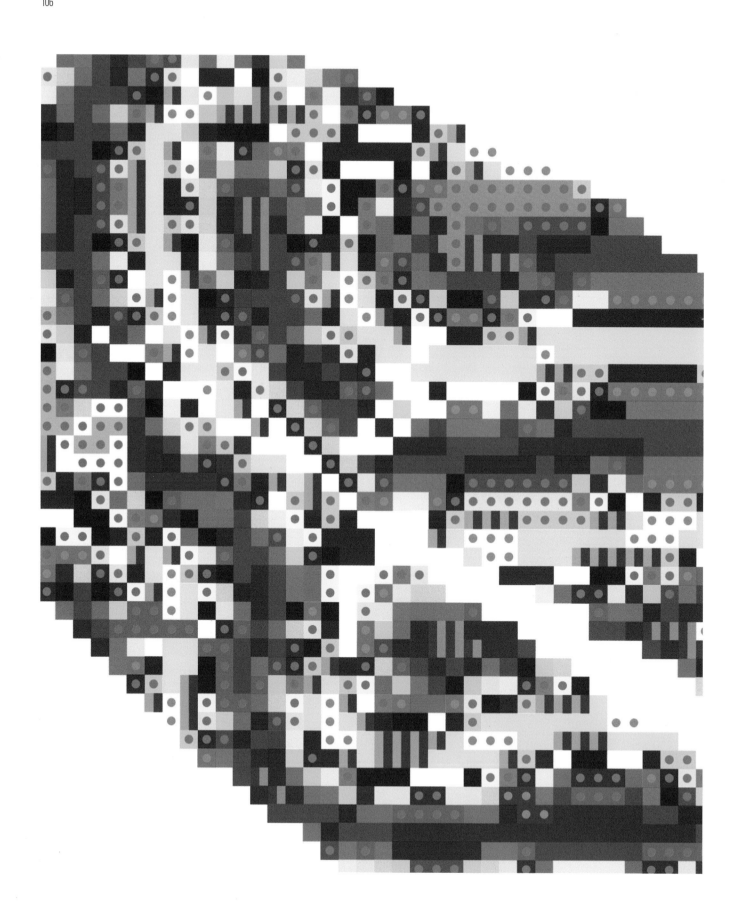

+ The term speculative is often used pejoratively–particularly when it is levied against design–to describe something without rigor, or that is naïve, or too idealistic. You have described yourself as an outsider on the inside, specifically as it relates to your work with synthetic biology. It seems that there is actually great value in the unknown – that really interesting outcomes emerge precisely because you're not an expert.

I come at all my projects as an amateur. I got involved in synthetic biology as an amateur and I became increasingly knowledgeable, but I was never a synthetic biologist. With *Pollinator Pathmaker* I have had to learn a lot again! I am not a gardener, I didn't know anything about bees, moths, or butterflies; about which plants, how to plant them, when to plant them, what works together, what's a perennial, what's an annual, what's going to be hardy, or how to create an algorithm or an interactive website.

Even though there are many more people who know more about gardening than about synthetic biology, it's daunting to get involved when you all you know is that you don't know. By learning along the way, you can communicate to other newcomers with empathy, and you can also ask questions that experts no longer remember as complex, or may not have noticed before, since you are bringing a different knowledge to theirs. This purposeful naïveté is incredibly useful. Constantly questioning everything. To ask, "Well okay, how does this work?" and, "What is this?" Childlike curiosity and admitting that I need to learn is useful and I think also offers a sense of optimism and hopefulness.

However, for me what is essential, is that the work is rooted in truth. *Designing for the Sixth Extinction* is a fiction, but it is informed by research in synthetic biology, such as on expanded genetic codes, as well as the political discussions happening around synthetic biology and conservation, and controversial ecological practices such as biodiversity offsetting. That is the framework the project sits on. My accumulation of knowledge from disparate fields along the way informs the work. The joy for me in making this kind of work are the moments where I get to learn from and talk with experts. That is such a privilege and a pleasure.

All of this ties together in my curiosity about the idea of hope. Why are humans optimistic? Even when things are terrible, humans are able to imagine otherwise. It's what Ernst Bloch writes about in *The Principle of Hope*–written in the 1930s in the darkest times–this idea that humans have an intrinsic hopefulness. I find it fascinating that we can be deeply pessimistic about the future of the environment and biodiversity, but there is still optimism that things could or at least *should* be otherwise. Even if we think it's terrible, we still must try. My shift toward environmental artworks feels like the most useful thing I can do to be hopeful.

Opposite: Digital rendering of Eden Project Edition Garden 1 (pixel view) from *Pollinator Pathmaker* (2021).

IMAGE CREDITS

Endpapers

"Artist's impression of the interior of an O'Neill cylinder: Endcap View with Suspension Bridge" by Donald Davis/NASA, public domain.

Piscinarii: The Fishpond Speculators of Rome

p. 4–5: "Roman Villa of Pisões, Lusitania, Portugal" (2014) by Carole Raddato, used under CC BY SA 2.0 license via Wikimedia Commons (altered).

p. 6: Map by Jing Qin (2021), used with permission.

p. 8: "Sperlonga Hill View" (2011) by Casey Lance Brown, used with permission.

The Measured Line and the Quantification of Space

p. 12–13: "The Mètre étalon at 36, rue de Vaugirard, Paris" by Airair used under CC BY SA 4.0 license via Wikimedia Commons.

p. 15: "Usage des nouvelles mesures" (ca. 1800) by unknown, public domain (altered).

Toward a Scientific Imaginary

p. 16–17: "Whipple Section Cut" (1854) by William P. Blake & Jules Marcou, Army Topographical Corps of Engineers, public domain.

p. 21: Landscape lithographs by unknown, from the Chicago Newberry Library collection, public domain.

p. 22–23: "Topographic Timeline," Army Topographical Corps of Engineers, public domain.

Centering the Fringe

p. 26–35: Images by Jonah Susskind, used with permission.

The Plane Table – A Tool of Speculation

p. 36: "Plane Table work in Southeast Alaska, Crew off Explorer" (1921) by unknown, public domain (cropped).

p. 38–39: "Scoring the Malecon" (2008) by Alecsandra Trofin, Sheryl Lam, Ezmira Peraj, and Leo Xian, used with permission via author (cropped and scaled).

p. 41: "Diachronic Garden" (2016) by Sarah Comfort and Chiara Fingland, used with permission via author.

p. 43: Selection from "Plane Table work in Southeast Alaska, Crew off Explorer" (1921) by unknown, public domain (cropped).

Futuring: A Conversation

p. 44: Image by Zihan Zuo, used with permission.

Dark Speculation

p. 56: "Blade Runner or Beijing?" by unknown via imgur.com.

Subject v. Method

p. 58: Image by Yang Du (2019), used with permission via author.

p. 60: Image by Anni Lei (2018), used with permission via author.

p. 61: Images by Zuzanna Drozdz (2019), used with permission via author.

p. 62: Images by Shuhan Liu (2018), used with permission via author.

p. 63: Images by Farre Nixon (2018), used with permission via author.

p. 65: Image by Mingyan Sun & Fangyuan Sheng (2020), used with permission via author (top); image by Aaron Stone & Keke Huang (2020), used with permission via author (bottom).

p. 66: Image by Bingjian Liu & Yufei Yan (2020), used with permission via author.

Everyday Space

p. 68–69: "Everyday Space" (2022) by Helen Yuchen Han, used with permission.

p. 70–77: Images courtesy of the Moscow Design Museum, used with permission via author.

Why? Why Not?

p. 78: Background image of *The Garden of Earthly Delights* by Hieronymus Bosch (ca. 1500), public domain via Wikimedia Commons.

p. 80–85: Images courtesy of the Why Factory, used with permission via author.

Afrofuturism: Collapsing Liminal Space

p. 86–87: "Afrofuturism" (2022) by Helen Yuchen Han, used with permission.

p. 93: "Door of No Return" (2007) by Angela Sevin, used under CC BY 2.0 license via flickr.com.

In Conversation with Alexandra Daisy Ginsberg

p. 94: Portrait of Alexandra Daisy Ginsberg, used with permission via author (altered).

p. 99: "Herbicide Gourd" (2009) illustration by Siôn Ap Tomas from *Growth Assembly* by Daisy Ginsberg and Sascha Pohflepp, used with permission.

p. 100: "Plant Icons" by Alexandra Daisy Ginsberg from *Pollinator Pathmaker* (2021), used with permission.

p. 102: *The Wilding of Mars* (2019) by Alexandra Daisy Ginsberg, used with permission (top); "The *E. chromi* Scatolog" from *E. chromi* (2009) by Alexandra Daisy Ginsberg and James King with the University of Cambridge 2009 iGEM team, used with permission (bottom).

p. 105: "Self-inflating Antipathogenic Membrane Pump" from *Designing for the Sixth Extinction* (2013–2015) by Alexandra Daisy Ginsberg.

p. 106: "Pixel View" (2021) by Alexandra Daisy Ginsberg from *Pollinator Pathmaker*, digital rendering of Eden Project Edition Garden 1, used with permission.

p.108: "Red Robot" from the Moscow Design Museum collection, used with permission via Alexandra Sankova.

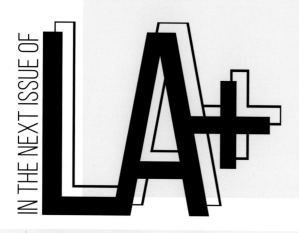

How can design be used to challenge the status quo, to interrupt the jargon, to disrupt and redirect ecological and socio-economic flows? LA+ Journal's fourth international design ideas competition invited designers to take an established place and design something to productively interrupt both its cultural and spatial context. What does this mean? It means injecting something different into a given context to effect new meanings and new functions. It means questioning what design does, who it's designed for, what it looks like, and what it means.

Issue #17 brings you the results of the **LA+ INTERRUPTION** design competition. As well as showcasing the award-winning designs and a comprehensive Salon des Refusés, LA+ INTERRUPTION will feature an essay on the theme and interviews with jurors Fiona Raby, Martin Rein-Cano, Mark Raggatt, Rania Ghosn, and Jason Zhisen Ho.

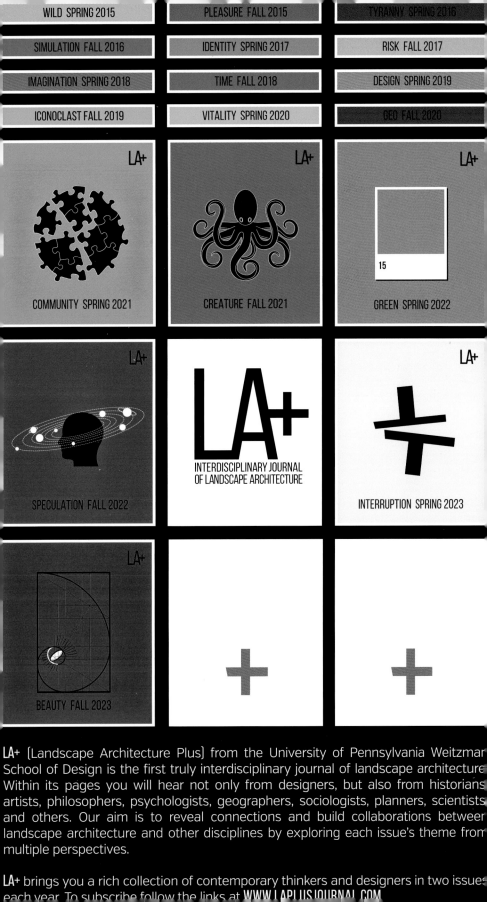

WILD SPRING 2015	PLEASURE FALL 2015	TYRANNY SPRING 2016
SIMULATION FALL 2016	IDENTITY SPRING 2017	RISK FALL 2017
IMAGINATION SPRING 2018	TIME FALL 2018	DESIGN SPRING 2019
ICONOCLAST FALL 2019	VITALITY SPRING 2020	GEO FALL 2020

COMMUNITY SPRING 2021

CREATURE FALL 2021

15

GREEN SPRING 2022

SPECULATION FALL 2022

LA+
INTERDISCIPLINARY JOURNAL
OF LANDSCAPE ARCHITECTURE

INTERRUPTION SPRING 2023

BEAUTY FALL 2023

LA+ (Landscape Architecture Plus) from the University of Pennsylvania Weitzman School of Design is the first truly interdisciplinary journal of landscape architecture. Within its pages you will hear not only from designers, but also from historians, artists, philosophers, psychologists, geographers, sociologists, planners, scientists, and others. Our aim is to reveal connections and build collaborations between landscape architecture and other disciplines by exploring each issue's theme from multiple perspectives.

LA+ brings you a rich collection of contemporary thinkers and designers in two issues each year. To subscribe follow the links at WWW.LAPLUSJOURNAL.COM